ADOBE PHOTOSHOP 2025 USER GUIDE

Your Step-by-Step Guide with Illustrated Manual with Tips, Tricks, and Shortcuts

Table of Contents

Introduction   9

    Who This Book Is For 9

    How to Use This Book...10

    What's New in Photoshop 2025?.......................................10

    Conventions Used in This Book..11

Downloading, Installing, and Setting Up 12

    1.1 System Requirements for Photoshop 2025 12

    1.2 Downloading Photoshop 2025 from Adobe Creative Cloud 14

    1.3 Installing Photoshop 2025..15

    1.4 Launching Photoshop and Activating Your License 16

    1.5 Setting Up Your Preferences for Optimal Performance 17

    1.6 Updating Photoshop 2025 25

    1.7 Using Generative AI Effectively..................................25

Navigating the Photoshop Workspace 27

    2.1 The Welcome Screen and Home Screen 27

    2.2 The Photoshop Interface 28

    2.3 The Menu Bar: Accessing Photoshop's Commands 28

    2.4 The Options Bar: Contextual Tool Settings 29

    2.5 The Tools Panel: Your Essential Toolkit 29

    2.6 Understanding and Managing Panels 31

    2.7 Working with Multiple Documents 32

    2.8 Customizing Your Workspace for Efficiency.............33

    2.9 Using Workspaces and Creating Your Own 33

Understanding Images and Color 35

    3.1 Raster vs. Vector Graphics: What's the Difference? ...35

    3.2 Image Resolution and Size: Pixels, PPI, and DPI Explained 36

    3.3 Common Image File Formats (JPEG, PNG, TIFF, GIF, PSD, etc.)....................37

    3.4 Color Modes: RGB, CMYK, Grayscale, and More 39

    3.5 Bit Depth: 8-bit, 16-bit, and 32-bit Explained 40

    3.6 Color Profiles and Color Management Basics 41

    3.7 Introduction to Photoshop Generative AI Features......42

Mastering Layers 44

    4.1 What are Layers and Why are They Important? 44

4.2 The Layers Panel: Your Layer Control Center 45

4.3 Creating, Duplicating, and Deleting Layers 46

4.4 Naming and Organizing Layers with Groups 46

4.5 Layer Blending Modes: Creating Unique Effects 47

4.6 Layer Opacity and Fill: Controlling Transparency 49

4.7 Layer Styles: Adding Depth and Dimension 50

4.8 Clipping Masks: Confining Effects to Specific Layers 52

4.9 Layer Masks: Non-Destructive Editing 53

4.10 Smart Objects: Preserving Image Quality 54

4.11 Introduction to AI-Powered Layer Management 55

Selections and Masking 57

5.1 The Importance of Accurate Selections 57

5.2 Marquee Tools: Rectangular, Elliptical, Single Row, Single Column 58

5.3 Lasso Tools: Freehand, Polygonal, and Magnetic 59

5.4 Quick Selection Tool and Magic Wand Tool 60

5.5 Object Selection Tool: Harnessing AI for Selection 62

5.6 Select Subject and Select and Mask Workspace 62

5.7 Refining Selections with the Refine Edge Brush 64

5.8 Saving and Loading Selections 65

5.9 Creating and Editing Layer Masks 66

5.10 Vector Masks: For Precision Edits 67

5.11 Advanced Masking Techniques 68

5.12 Using AI to Generate Complex Masks 69

Creating and Importing Documents 70

6.1 Creating a New Document: Setting Up Size, Resolution, and Color Mode 70

6.2 Using Presets and Templates 72

6.3 Opening Existing Images 73

6.4 Importing Images from Scanners and Cameras 73

6.5 Placing Images as Smart Objects 75

6.6 Working with Artboards for Multi-Screen Design 76

6.7 Saving Your Work: File Formats and Options 78

6.8 Importing and Using AI-Generated Assets 81

Working with Smart Objects 85

7.1 What are Smart Objects and Why Use Them? 85

7.2 Creating Smart Objects 86

7.3 Editing the Contents of a Smart Object 87

7.4 Replacing the Contents of a Smart Object 88

7.5 Converting Smart Objects Back to Layers 89

7.6 Benefits of Smart Objects for Non-Destructive Editing........................90

7.7 Using Smart Objects with Filters and Adjustments..............................91

Essential Retouching Tools 94

8.1 The Healing Brush: Removing Blemishes and Imperfections 94

8.2 The Spot Healing Brush: Quick Fixes with AI 96

8.3 The Patch Tool: Seamlessly Replacing Areas 97

8.4 The Clone Stamp Tool: Duplicating Image Areas...............................98

8.5 The Content-Aware Move Tool: Repositioning Elements Intelligently..........100

8.6 The Red Eye Tool: Correcting Red Eye in Photos.............................101

8.7 Blur, Sharpen, and Smudge Tools: Fine-Tuning Details 102

8.8 Dodge and Burn Tools: Lightening and Darkening Areas 103

8.9 The Sponge Tool: Adjusting Saturation 104

8.10 Advanced Retouching with Frequency Separation.........................105

Color Correction and Adjustment...107

9.1 Understanding Histograms: Analyzing Image Tones.........................107

9.2 Brightness/Contrast: Adjusting Overall Tonality 109

9.3 Levels: Fine-Tuning Highlights, Midtones, and Shadows..................110

9.4 Curves: Advanced Tonal Control 111

9.5 Exposure: Correcting Overexposed and Underexposed Images 113

9.6 Vibrance and Saturation: Enhancing Colors.....................................114

9.7 Hue/Saturation: Shifting and Modifying Colors................................115

9.8 Color Balance: Correcting Color Casts 116

9.9 Black & White: Creating Stunning Monochrome Images..................117

9.10 Photo Filter: Adding Color Tints and Effects..................................118

9.11 Channel Mixer: Advanced Color Adjustments.................................119

9.12 Invert, Posterize, Threshold, Gradient Map, Selective Color 120

9.13 Match Color, Replace Color, Equalize...120

9.14 HDR Toning 123

9.15 Shadows/Highlights 124

9.16 Using AI for Automatic Color Correction..125

Filters and Effects...127

10.1 An Overview of Photoshop's Filter Gallery.....................................127

10.2 Applying Filters Non-Destructively with Smart Filters.................................128

10.3 Blur Filters: Gaussian Blur, Motion Blur, Radial Blur, and More 130

10.4 Sharpen Filters: Unsharp Mask, Smart Sharpen, and More 131

10.5 Noise Filters: Add Noise, Reduce Noise, and More..133

10.6 Stylize Filters: Find Edges, Emboss, Wind, and More 134

10.7 Distort Filters: Ripple, Wave, Twirl, and More...136

10.8 Render Filters: Clouds, Fibers, Lens Flare, Lighting Effects.......................137

10.9 Neural Filters: AI-Powered Image Transformations....................................139

10.10 Working with Third-Party Filters 148

10.11 Using Generative AI to Create Custom Filters...149

Transforming and Manipulating Images 151

11.1 Cropping and Straightening Images 151

11.2 Resizing Images: Image Size vs. Canvas Size 152

11.3 Rotating and Flipping Images...154

11.4 Free Transform: Scaling, Rotating, Skewing, Distorting, and Perspective.....155

11.5 Warp Tool: Advanced Image Manipulation..156

11.6 Puppet Warp: Precise Control over Image Elements 157

11.7 Content-Aware Scale: Intelligently Resizing Images....................................159

11.8 Perspective Warp: Correcting and Adjusting Perspective 160

Working with Type 161

12.1 The Type Tool: Adding Text to Your Images 161

12.2 Formatting Text: Font, Size, Color, Alignment, and More 162

12.3 Character and Paragraph Panels: Advanced Text Options..........................163

12.4 Creating and Editing Text on a Path 164

12.5 Warping Text for Creative Effects 166

12.6 Using Type as a Mask 166

12.7 Working with 3D Text...167

Painting and Brushes 169

13.1 The Brush Tool: An Overview 169

13.2 Brush Presets and Customizing Brushes...170

13.3 Brush Dynamics: Shape, Scattering, Texture, and More 172

13.4 The Mixer Brush Tool: Simulating Real-World Painting 174

13.5 The Pencil Tool: For Hard-Edged Lines 175

13.6 The Color Replacement Tool 176

13.7 Creating and Using Custom Brushes 177

13.8 Using a Graphics Tablet for Pressure Sensitivity.................................179

13.9 Exploring AI-Generated Brushes and Textures..................................180

Introduction to 3D in Photoshop..182

14.1 Overview of Photoshop's 3D Capabilities..................................182

14.2 Creating and Importing 3D Objects..183

14.3 Manipulating 3D Objects in the Workspace.............................183

14.4 Working with 3D Text 185

14.5 Applying Materials and Textures to 3D Objects 185

14.6 Lighting and Rendering 3D Scenes 186

14.7 Exporting 3D Models 187

Automating Tasks with Actions..189

15.1 What are Actions and How Can They Save You Time? 189

15.2 Recording Actions: Step-by-Step Guide..................................190

15.3 Playing Actions: Automating Your Workflow 192

15.4 Managing Actions: Organizing, Editing, and Deleting 192

15.5 Creating Conditional Actions..193

15.6 Batch Processing: Applying Actions to Multiple Files 194

15.7 Using Droplets for Easy Automation 196

Preparing Images for Web and Print...197

16.1 Optimizing Images for the Web: File Size and Quality 197

16.2 Using the Save for Web (Legacy) Dialog.................................198

16.3 Creating Animated GIFs 200

16.4 Preparing Images for Print: Resolution, Color Mode, and File Format........201

16.5 Working with Print Service Providers 203

16.6 Soft Proofing: Previewing Colors for Print..............................204

16.7 Exporting with Generative AI for Enhanced Quality 205

Troubleshooting and Best Practices...207

17.1 Common Photoshop Problems and How to Solve Them...............207

17.2 Performance Optimization Tips...209

17.3 Keyboard Shortcuts for Efficient Workflow.............................210

17.4 Non-Destructive Editing: Best Practices 212

17.5 Staying Organized: File Management and Naming Conventions...................213

17.6 Backing Up Your Work 214

17.7 Resources for Further Learning..215

Keyboard Shortcuts..216

Menu Shortcuts 216

Tool Shortcuts 225

Panel Shortcuts 225

Filter Shortcuts 226

Customizing Shortcuts...226

Glossary of Terms 228

Introduction

Welcome to the exciting world of Adobe Photoshop 2025! Whether you're just starting your creative journey or you're a seasoned professional looking to master the latest tools and techniques, this book is your comprehensive guide to unlocking the full potential of this incredibly powerful software. We're thrilled to embark on this visual adventure with you, exploring everything from the fundamentals to the most cutting-edge features that Photoshop 2025 has to offer.

Adobe Photoshop has long been the industry standard for image editing and manipulation, and the 2025 version continues to push the boundaries of what's possible. With a focus on streamlined workflows, AI-powered enhancements, and even more creative possibilities, Photoshop 2025 is a game-changer. This book will not only teach you *how* to use the software but also *why* certain techniques are effective, empowering you to make informed creative decisions and develop your own unique style.

Who This Book Is For

This book is designed to be your go-to resource, regardless of your current skill level. We've carefully structured the content to cater to a wide range of users:

- **Beginners:** If you're new to Photoshop, don't worry! We'll start with the basics, guiding you through the interface, fundamental concepts, and essential tools. You'll build a solid foundation that will allow you to confidently tackle more complex techniques as you progress.
- **Intermediate Users:** For those with some Photoshop experience, this book will help you refine your skills, discover new workflows, and delve deeper into advanced features like masking, smart objects, and non-destructive editing. You'll learn how to leverage the power of Photoshop more efficiently and creatively.
- **Advanced Users and Professionals:** Even seasoned pros will find valuable insights and techniques in this book. We'll explore the latest AI-powered tools, advanced retouching methods, 3D capabilities, and automation strategies to help you stay at the forefront of the industry and optimize your workflow.
- **Anyone looking to use Photoshop's Generative AI Features:** If your interest is in image generation, manipulation, and creation, this book has you covered!

How to Use This Book

This book is designed to be both a comprehensive tutorial and a handy reference guide. You can choose to work through it sequentially, building your knowledge step-by-step, or jump directly to specific chapters that address your immediate needs.

- **Follow Along:** Each chapter is packed with practical examples, clear instructions, and illustrative screenshots. We encourage you to follow along on your own computer, experimenting with the tools and techniques as you read.
- **Practice Makes Perfect:** Don't be afraid to experiment! The best way to learn Photoshop is by doing. Try applying the techniques you learn to your own images and projects.
- **Take Advantage of Online Resources:** The world of digital art and design is always evolving. We've included a list of helpful online resources in Chapter 17 that you can explore to expand your knowledge and stay up-to-date.
- **Use the Index and Glossary:** If you're looking for information on a specific tool or technique, the comprehensive index at the back of the book will quickly point you in the right direction. The glossary provides definitions of key terms.

What's New in Photoshop 2025?

Photoshop 2025 introduces a range of exciting new features and enhancements designed to boost your creativity and streamline your workflow. Here are some of the highlights we'll be exploring in detail:

- **Enhanced Neural Filters:** Building on the success of previous versions, Photoshop 2025's Neural Filters leverage the power of artificial intelligence to perform complex image transformations with unprecedented ease. Expect even more realistic results, finer control, and new filters that will spark your imagination, such as Enhanced Image Restoration, Generative Object Removal, and Style Fusion.
- **Next-Generation Content-Aware Tools:** Content-Aware Fill, Content-Aware Scale, and other related tools have been significantly improved, utilizing advanced AI algorithms to deliver more seamless and believable results when removing objects, resizing images, or filling in missing areas. This includes a new Context-Aware mode, which allows the user to give the AI additional context clues for a more refined result.
- **Improved Object Selection and Masking:** Photoshop 2025 makes selecting and masking objects even faster and more accurate, thanks to enhanced edge detection and AI-powered refinement tools. The new One-Click Mask All feature can identify and generate masks for all detectable objects in an image in a single step.
- **Streamlined Cloud Integration:** Collaboration and file management are smoother than ever with enhanced integration with Adobe Creative Cloud. Share files, gather feedback, and work seamlessly across devices.
- **Generative AI Capabilities:** Photoshop 2025 takes a leap forward in generative AI, allowing users to create variations of images, add elements, and even generate entire scenes from text prompts or sketches. A new feature, Generative Expand, allows users to prompt image generation beyond the image's original canvas.
- **Performance Optimizations:** Enjoy a faster and more responsive editing experience thanks to under-the-hood performance improvements that make working with large files and complex projects smoother than ever.

Conventions Used in This Book

To ensure clarity and consistency, we've used the following conventions throughout this book:

- **Boldface** type indicates menu commands, dialog box options, and panel names (e.g., "Go to **File > Open**" or "Click on the **Layers** panel").
- *Italics* are used for emphasis, new terms, and file names (e.g., "This is a *non-destructive* edit" or "Open the file named *image.psd*").
- Monospaced type is used for code, keyboard shortcuts, and text you should type (e.g., "Press Ctrl+S (Windows) or Cmd+S (Mac) to save").
- Notes, Tips, and Warnings are highlighted in separate boxes to draw your attention to important information.

Downloading, Installing, and Setting Up

Before you can dive into the exciting world of digital image editing with Photoshop 2025, you need to get the software up and running on your computer. This chapter will guide you through the process of downloading, installing, and activating your copy of Photoshop 2025. We'll also cover the essential system requirements to ensure a smooth and efficient editing experience.

1.1 System Requirements for Photoshop 2025

Adobe Photoshop 2025 is a powerful application with advanced features, including AI-powered tools that require significant processing power. To get the most out of it, your computer needs to meet certain minimum system requirements. While the software might run on systems that fall below these specifications, you'll likely experience performance issues, especially when working with large files or complex projects.

Here are the recommended system requirements for Photoshop 2025:

Windows:
- **Processor:** Intel® or AMD processor with 64-bit support; 2 GHz or faster processor with SSE 4.2 or later
- **Operating System:** Windows 10 64-bit (version 1909) or later; LTSC versions are not supported. Windows 11 is fully supported and recommended for best results with Generative AI features.
- **RAM:** 8 GB of RAM (16 GB or more recommended)
- **Graphics Card:** GPU with DirectX 12 support and 4 GB of GPU memory for 4k displays and greater (8 GB recommended). For optimal performance with Neural Filters and other AI-powered features, a dedicated graphics card with at least 6 GB of VRAM is strongly recommended.

- **Hard Disk Space:** 4 GB of available hard-disk space for installation; additional space required for scratch disks (SSD recommended). A fast SSD is highly recommended for both the application and as a dedicated scratch disk.
- **Monitor Resolution:** 1280 x 800 display at 100% UI scaling (1920 x 1080 display or greater recommended)
- **Internet:** Internet connection and registration are necessary for required software activation, validation of subscriptions, and access to online services.

macOS:
- **Processor:** Intel® processor with 64-bit support or Apple Silicon processor (M1, M2, or newer). Native Apple Silicon support provides significant performance gains.
- **Operating System:** macOS Monterey (version 12) or later (macOS Ventura or later recommended)
- **RAM:** 8 GB of RAM (16 GB or more recommended)
- **Graphics Card:** GPU with Metal support and 4 GB of GPU memory for 4k displays and greater (8 GB recommended). For optimal performance with AI features, a dedicated graphics card is strongly recommended. Apple Silicon's unified memory architecture generally provides excellent performance.
- **Hard Disk Space:** 4 GB of available hard-disk space for installation; additional space required for scratch disks (SSD recommended). As with Windows, a fast SSD is highly recommended.
- **Monitor Resolution:** 1280 x 800 display at 100% UI scaling (1920 x 1080 display or greater recommended)
- **Internet:** Internet connection and registration are necessary for required software activation, validation of subscriptions, and access to online services.

Important Notes:
- These are the *recommended* requirements. You may be able to run Photoshop 2025 with slightly lower specs, but performance may be affected, especially with demanding tasks.
- Features like Neural Filters and other AI tools rely heavily on GPU acceleration. A powerful graphics card will significantly improve their performance.
- Adobe frequently updates Photoshop, and system requirements may change. Always refer to the official Adobe website for the most up-to-date information.
- For users interested in using Photoshop's Generative AI features, a stable and fast internet connection is crucial, as these features often rely on cloud processing.

1.2 Downloading Photoshop 2025 from Adobe Creative Cloud

Photoshop 2025 is available through Adobe Creative Cloud, a subscription-based service that gives you access to Adobe's suite of creative applications, along with cloud storage, fonts, and other benefits. Here's how to download it:

1. **Create an Adobe ID (if you don't have one):** If you don't already have an Adobe ID, you'll need to create one. Visit the Adobe website (www.adobe.com) and click on

"Sign In" in the top right corner. Then, click on "Create an account" and follow the instructions.

2. **Choose a Creative Cloud Plan:** Adobe offers various Creative Cloud plans. You can choose a plan that includes only Photoshop or a plan that includes other applications like Lightroom, Illustrator, and Premiere Pro. Select the plan that best suits your needs and budget. Common options include:
   - **Photography Plan:** Includes Photoshop and Lightroom. Ideal for photographers.
   - **Single App Plan (Photoshop):** Only includes Photoshop.
   - **All Apps Plan:** Includes all Adobe creative applications. Best for users who need a wide range of creative tools.
   - **Free Trial:** Select the trial to get temporary access to the full version of Photoshop 2025 for 7 days.

3. **Download and Install the Creative Cloud Desktop App:** Once you've subscribed to a plan, you'll be prompted to download the Creative Cloud desktop application. This app is your central hub for managing your Adobe applications, updates, and cloud services.

4. **Sign In to the Creative Cloud App:** After installing the Creative Cloud app, launch it and sign in using your Adobe ID and password.

5. **Find and Install Photoshop 2025:** In the Creative Cloud app, you'll see a list of available applications. Locate "Photoshop 2025" (it might be listed under the "All Apps" tab or the "Photography" category, depending on your plan). Click the "Install" button next to it.

6. **Monitor the Download Progress:** The Creative Cloud app will show you the download progress. The download time will depend on your internet speed.

1.3 Installing Photoshop 2025

In most cases, the installation process will begin automatically after the download is complete. However, here's a general overview of the steps involved if you need to install manually or want to understand the process:

1. **Automatic Installation (Typical):** After downloading via the Creative Cloud desktop app, Photoshop 2025 will usually install automatically. You'll see a progress bar indicating the installation status.

2. **Manual Installation (If Needed):** If the installation doesn't start automatically, you might need to locate the downloaded installer file (usually in your "Downloads" folder) and double-click it to start the installation process.

3. **Follow the On-Screen Instructions:** The installer will guide you through the installation process. You may be asked to:
   - Accept the Adobe Software License Agreement.
   - Choose an installation location (the default location is usually recommended).
   - Optionally choose to install additional components (like language packs).

4. **Wait for the Installation to Complete:** The installation process may take several minutes, depending on your computer's speed.
5. **Launch Photoshop:** Once the installation is finished, you can launch Photoshop 2025 from the Creative Cloud app or from your computer's applications menu (Start Menu on Windows or Applications folder on macOS).

1.4 Launching Photoshop and Activating Your License

1. **Launch Photoshop 2025:** You can launch Photoshop in a few ways:
   - **From the Creative Cloud App:** Click the "Open" button next to Photoshop 2025 in the Creative Cloud app.
   - **From your Applications Menu:**
     - **Windows:** Click the Start Menu, then find and click on "Adobe Photoshop 2025."
     - **macOS:** Open the Applications folder and double-click on "Adobe Photoshop 2025."

2. **Sign In (If Prompted):** The first time you launch Photoshop, you'll likely be prompted to sign in with your Adobe ID and password. This activates your license and links the software to your Creative Cloud account. This also enables cloud features such as Generative AI.

3. **Explore the Welcome Screen:** After signing in, you'll see the Photoshop Welcome Screen (also known as the Home Screen). This screen provides quick access to recent files, tutorials, and options for creating new documents.

Congratulations! You've successfully downloaded, installed, and launched Adobe Photoshop 2025. You're now ready to start exploring the software and unleashing your creative potential. In the next chapter, we'll take a closer look at the Photoshop workspace and familiarize you with the essential tools and panels.

Now that Photoshop 2025 is installed, it's a good idea to take a few minutes to configure its preferences. While the default settings are generally suitable for most users, customizing them to your specific needs and hardware can significantly improve performance, streamline your workflow, and enhance your overall editing experience.

To access the Preferences dialog, go to:

- **Windows:** Edit > Preferences > General
- **macOS:** Photoshop > Preferences > General

You can also use the keyboard shortcut **Ctrl+K** (Windows) or **Cmd+K** (macOS) to quickly open the Preferences.

The Preferences dialog is organized into several categories, each containing various settings. Let's explore some of the most important ones for optimizing performance:

1.5.1 General Preferences

This section contains a mix of general settings. While most can be left at their default values, here are a couple to consider:

- **Image Interpolation:** This setting determines how Photoshop resizes images. **Bicubic Automatic** is generally a good choice, as Photoshop will choose the best bicubic method depending on whether you are enlarging or reducing an image. If you frequently enlarge images you might consider **Preserve Details 2.0**; though it is more resource intensive.
- **Legacy "New Document" Interface:** If you prefer the older New Document dialog from previous Photoshop versions, you can check this option.
- **Auto-Show the Home Screen:** If you'd rather go straight to the Photoshop workspace when launching the application or closing all open documents, uncheck this.
- **Use Shift Key for Tool Switch:** This allows you to cycle through tools that share the same shortcut key by pressing the shortcut key repeatedly. Some users prefer to use the Shift key to cycle through the tools instead.

1.5.2 Interface Preferences

These settings control the look and feel of the Photoshop workspace:

- **Color Theme:** Choose a color theme that's comfortable for your eyes. Darker themes are often preferred for extended editing sessions, while some prefer a lighter theme.
- **UI Scaling:** If you're using a high-resolution monitor, you can adjust the UI scaling to make the interface elements larger and easier to see. You can choose **Auto**, **100%**, or **200%**.
- **UI Font Size:** Adjust the size of the text in menus, panels, and dialogs.

1.5.3 Tools Preferences

This section offers options for customizing the behavior of various tools:

- **Zoom with Scroll Wheel:** Check this to zoom in and out using your mouse's scroll wheel. Highly recommended for faster navigation.
- **Flick Panning:** Allows you to quickly move around the image by clicking and dragging, like on a touch screen.
- **Double-Clicking the Hand tool will fit the image to the viewable area:** This is a useful shortcut to know and enables quick navigation.
- **Overscroll:** This allows you to pan past the normal bounds of your image. Some users like this, and others find it disconcerting.
- **Enable Gestures:** Enable or disable various multi-touch gestures if you have a touch-enabled device.
- **Show Tool Tips:** If you're new to Photoshop, it's helpful to leave this option checked. Tool tips provide brief descriptions of each tool when you hover over them.

1.5.4 Performance Preferences
This is arguably the most critical section for optimizing Photoshop's speed and efficiency:

- **Memory Usage:** This setting determines how much RAM Photoshop is allowed to use. By default, Photoshop is allocated a certain percentage of your available RAM. You can adjust the "Let Photoshop Use" slider to allocate more or less RAM.
  - **Increasing RAM allocation can significantly improve performance, especially when working with large files or multiple documents.** However, don't allocate all your RAM to Photoshop, as your operating system and other applications also need memory.
  - Generally, 70-85% is a good range for Photoshop. Monitor your system's memory usage while working in Photoshop to fine-tune this setting.

- **Graphics Processor Settings:** Make sure the "Use Graphics Processor" option is checked. This enables Photoshop to utilize your graphics card (GPU) for accelerated performance, especially for tasks like screen rendering, zooming, panning, and using GPU-accelerated filters like Neural Filters.
  - Click on **Advanced Settings** to further fine-tune GPU usage:

- **Drawing Mode:** Advanced generally provides the best performance, taking full advantage of your GPU. If you encounter display issues, you can try Normal or Basic.

- **Use OpenCL:** Enable this option to accelerate features like the Blur Gallery, Smart Sharpen, and Select and Mask.
  - **30 Bit Display:** Only check this if you have a monitor that supports 30-bit color.

- **History & Cache:**
  - **History States:** This determines the number of undo steps Photoshop remembers. Increasing the number of history states allows you to undo more actions but also consumes more memory and can slow down performance. A value between 50-100 is generally a good balance.

- **Cache Levels:** This setting affects how Photoshop stores image data in its cache. Higher cache levels can improve performance when working with large images, but they also require more disk space. The default value (4) is usually sufficient.
- **Cache Tile Size:** This setting determines the size of the image tiles that Photoshop uses for caching. Larger tile sizes can be faster for large images, but they also consume more memory. The default (1024K) is a good starting point.

1.5.5 Scratch Disks

Scratch disks are temporary storage spaces that Photoshop uses when it runs out of RAM. Think of them as an overflow valve for your computer's memory.

- **It is highly recommended to have a dedicated scratch disk that is separate from the drive where your operating system and Photoshop are installed.** Ideally, your scratch disk should be a fast SSD.
- **You can assign multiple scratch disks.** Photoshop will use them in the order they are listed. If one scratch disk fills up, Photoshop will start using the next one.
- To configure your scratch disks, check the boxes next to the drives you want to use and use the up and down arrows to change their priority.
- Having at least 25-50GB of free space available on your scratch disk is recommended.

1.5.6 Cursors

These settings control the appearance of your cursors:

- **Painting Cursors:** Choose between **Standard**, **Precise** (crosshairs), **Normal Brush Tip**, **Full Size Brush Tip**, or other options. "Normal Brush Tip" is often preferred as it shows the size and shape of your brush.
- **Other Cursors:** Choose between **Standard** or **Precise**.
- **Brush Preview Color:** You can change the color of the brush preview that appears when using certain tools.

1.5.7 Transparency & Gamut

These settings affect how transparency and out-of-gamut colors are displayed:

- **Transparency Settings:** You can customize the size and colors of the checkerboard pattern that Photoshop uses to indicate transparency.
- **Gamut Warning:** This option highlights areas in your image that are outside the printable color gamut of a specific color profile. You can change the color used for the warning.

1.5.8 Units & Rulers

These settings determine the units of measurement used in Photoshop:

- **Rulers:** Choose your preferred unit for rulers (e.g., pixels, inches, centimeters). Pixels are generally recommended for screen-based work, while inches or centimeters are more common for print.
- **Type:** Choose your preferred unit for type (e.g., points, pixels, millimeters). Points are standard for print, while pixels are common for web design.

- **Column Size:** These are legacy settings related to newspaper column layouts.
- **Point/Pica Size:** Choose between PostScript (72 points/inch) or Traditional (72.27 points/inch). PostScript is the more common standard.
- **New Document Preset Resolution:** Set the default resolution for new documents created for Print or Screen.

1.5.9 Guides, Grid & Slices

These settings control the appearance of guides, grids, and slices:
- **Guides:** Customize the color and style (solid or dashed lines) of guides.
- **Grid:** Customize the color, style, and spacing of the grid. The grid can be helpful for aligning elements precisely.
- **Slices:** Customize the color of slice lines. Slices are used for dividing images into smaller sections for web optimization.

Important Note: Remember that preference changes are generally applied after you click "OK" in the Preferences dialog. Some changes may require you to restart Photoshop to take full effect.

By taking the time to configure these preferences, you'll be well on your way to a smoother, more efficient, and more personalized Photoshop experience. In the next sections of this chapter, we'll continue setting up Photoshop by exploring how to work with plugins and ultimately how to setup your workspace!

1.5.10 Plug-Ins

Plug-ins are add-ons that extend the functionality of Photoshop. They can add new features, filters, tools, and automation capabilities.

- **Show All Filter Gallery groups and names:** This will show all filters, including disabled ones.
- **Internet Connection Settings:** If you are behind a proxy server, you can enter your proxy settings here.
- **Enable Remote Fonts:** This enables fonts that are not installed on your system but are available through a connected service such as Adobe Fonts.
- **Legacy Extensions:** This allows extensions that were created for older versions of Photoshop to be used. These should be avoided if possible, as they can cause stability and performance issues.
- **Allow Extensions to Connect to the Internet:** This setting, enabled by default, allows extensions to perform necessary functions that require an internet connection.
- **Load Extension Panels:** This option, checked by default, allows you to load third-party extensions.

Where to Find Plug-Ins:

- **Adobe Exchange:** A marketplace for extensions, many specifically designed for Creative Cloud apps.
- **Developer Websites:** Many software developers offer Photoshop plug-ins directly from their websites.

Installing Plug-Ins:

- Many plug-ins come with their own installers.
- Some plug-ins need to be manually copied into the Photoshop Plug-Ins folder. The location of this folder varies depending on your operating system and Photoshop version, but it's generally found within the Photoshop application directory.

Managing Plug-Ins:

You can enable, disable, and manage your installed plug-ins within the Creative Cloud desktop app.

1.5.11 Type

These preferences affect how Photoshop handles text:

- **Show Font Names in English:** If you're working with fonts in multiple languages, unchecking this option will display font names in their native scripts.
- **Use ESC key to commit text:** By default, pressing the ESC key while editing text will cancel your changes. Checking this box will instead commit the changes.

- **Enable Missing Glyph Protection:** This will display a warning if you try to use a character that is not available in the selected font.
- **Enable Type layer glyph alternates:** This will allow you to access alternate characters in fonts that support them.
- **Fill new type layers with placeholder text:** When checked, new type layers will automatically be filled with "Lorem Ipsum" placeholder text, which can be helpful for visualizing layouts.
- **Use Smart Quotes:** This automatically replaces straight quotes with typographically correct curly quotes.

1.5.12 3D

Note: Adobe is gradually phasing out 3D features in Photoshop. While they might still be present in Photoshop 2025, their functionality might be limited, and they may be removed in future versions. This section is kept for legacy purposes.

These settings control various aspects of Photoshop's 3D capabilities. If you don't work with 3D, you can generally leave these settings at their defaults. If you do use 3D features, consider these settings:

- **RAM Available to 3D:** Similar to the general Performance settings, this slider lets you dedicate RAM specifically to 3D operations.
- **Detailed Options:** Here, you can adjust settings like the quality of interactive rendering, ray tracing, and shadows.

1.5.13 Technology Previews

This section is exciting because it allows you to enable and test experimental features that are still under development. Keep in mind that these features might be unstable or change significantly before their official release.

- **Deactivate Native Canvas:** This disables certain optimizations related to on-screen rendering. Only disable this feature if specifically instructed to by Adobe support.
- **Enable Content Credentials (Beta):** When enabled, you can attach attribution information to your images, which can help with provenance and authenticity verification.
- **Enable Native Canvas Rulers:** This enables a more modern ruler implementation. Try toggling it on and off to see which version you prefer.
- **Other Preview Features:** Photoshop 2025 might include other technology previews, such as AI-powered tools or workflow enhancements. Check the descriptions carefully and enable them at your own discretion. Adobe often provides feedback mechanisms for technology previews so you can report bugs or suggest improvements.

1.5.14 Product Improvement

- **Participate:** This option allows Adobe to collect anonymous usage data to help improve Photoshop. You can choose to participate or not based on your privacy preferences.

1.6 Updating Photoshop 2025

Adobe regularly releases updates to Photoshop, adding new features, improving performance, and fixing bugs. It's crucial to keep your software up to date to get the best possible experience.

How to Update:
1. **Creative Cloud Desktop App:** The Creative Cloud desktop app is the easiest way to update Photoshop. It will notify you when updates are available.
2. **Check for Updates:** In the Creative Cloud app, go to the "Apps" tab and click on "Updates" in the sidebar.
3. **Install Updates:** If an update for Photoshop 2025 is available, you'll see an "Update" button next to it. Click the button to download and install the update.
4. **Automatic Updates (Optional):** You can configure the Creative Cloud app to automatically download and install updates in the background. Go to File > Preferences (or Creative Cloud > Preferences on macOS) in the Creative Cloud app and adjust the settings under the "Apps" tab.
5. **Important Note:** It's generally a good idea to save any open work in Photoshop before installing an update, just in case something goes wrong.

1.7 Using Generative AI Effectively

Photoshop 2025's Generative AI features, such as those found in Neural Filters and Content-Aware tools, represent a significant leap forward in image editing. Here are some tips for using them effectively:

- **Understand the Limitations:** While AI is powerful, it's not magic. Be aware of the limitations of these tools and be prepared to refine the results manually when needed.
- **Provide Clear Input:** When using features that rely on text prompts or selections, be as clear and specific as possible to guide the AI towards your desired outcome.
- **Experiment with Settings:** Most Generative AI tools offer adjustable parameters. Experiment with different settings to see how they affect the results.
- **Iterate and Refine:** Don't be afraid to undo and try again. Generative AI often works best through an iterative process of experimentation and refinement.
- **Combine with Traditional Techniques:** Generative AI tools are most powerful when used in conjunction with Photoshop's traditional editing tools. Use them to get a head start, then refine the details with manual adjustments.
- **Use High-Quality Source Images:** The quality of your input images will significantly impact the quality of the output generated by AI.
- **Stay Ethical:** Be mindful of the ethical implications of using AI to manipulate images, especially when it comes to representing people or events. Be transparent about your use of AI and strive to use these powerful tools responsibly.

- **Stay Informed:** The field of AI is rapidly evolving. Keep up with the latest developments and best practices by following industry news and resources.

This concludes Chapter 1. You've now successfully installed Photoshop 2025, configured its preferences for optimal performance, and learned how to keep it updated. You're also ready to start exploring the exciting world of Generative AI. In the next chapter, we'll dive into the Photoshop workspace and get acquainted with the essential tools and panels that will be your companions on your creative journey!

Navigating the Photoshop Workspace

Welcome to the Photoshop workspace! This is where the magic happens. In this chapter, we'll take a guided tour of the Photoshop interface, exploring its various components and learning how to customize it to suit your workflow. By the end of this chapter, you'll be comfortable navigating the workspace and ready to start creating.

2.1 The Welcome Screen and Home Screen

When you first launch Photoshop 2025, you'll be greeted by the **Welcome Screen** (also known as the **Home Screen**). This screen serves as a central hub, providing quick access to:

- **Recent Files:** A list of recently opened documents, allowing you to quickly pick up where you left off. You can view them as thumbnails or as a list.
- **Learn:** Links to tutorials and learning resources from Adobe, perfect for both beginners and experienced users looking to expand their skills.
- **Lightroom Photos:** If you use Adobe Lightroom, you can access your synced photos directly from the Home Screen.
- **Cloud Documents:** Access files you have saved to Adobe's Creative Cloud.
- **Create New:** A button to create a new Photoshop document from scratch.
- **Open:** A button to open an existing image file from your computer.
- **Your Work:** This tab allows you to access your recent files, files shared with you, deleted files, and Lightroom photos.
- **What's New:** This tab showcases the latest features and updates in Photoshop 2025.
- **Learn:** This tab takes you to a variety of tutorials and learning resources, including in-app tutorials and links to online content.

You can customize the Home Screen to some extent by going to **Preferences > General** and unchecking **"Auto-show the Home Screen."** Doing so will take you directly to the main Photoshop workspace when you launch the application or when no documents are open.

2.2 The Photoshop Interface

Once you create a new document or open an existing one, you'll enter the main Photoshop workspace. Let's break down the key elements:

- **Menu Bar:** Located at the very top of the screen, the Menu Bar contains drop-down menus that provide access to virtually all of Photoshop's commands, organized by category (File, Edit, Image, Layer, Type, Select, Filter, 3D, View, Window, Help).
- **Options Bar:** Just below the Menu Bar, the Options Bar is context-sensitive. It changes depending on the currently selected tool, displaying relevant settings and options for that tool.

- **Tools Panel:** Typically docked to the left side of the screen, the Tools Panel contains Photoshop's essential tools for selecting, painting, editing, and manipulating images.
- **Document Window:** The central area where your image is displayed. You can have multiple document windows open simultaneously.
- **Panels:** Docked to the right side by default, panels provide access to a wide range of functionalities and settings, such as Layers, Adjustments, Properties, History, and more.
- **Status Bar:** Located at the bottom of the Document Window, the Status Bar displays useful information about the current file, such as zoom level, document size, and the active tool.

2.3 The Menu Bar: Accessing Photoshop's Commands

The Menu Bar is your gateway to the vast majority of Photoshop's features and commands. Here's a brief overview of each menu:

- **File:** Create, open, save, import, export, and print documents. Also includes options for automating tasks and managing file information.
- **Edit:** Undo, redo, cut, copy, paste, transform, and fill selections. Also contains preferences and color settings.
- **Image:** Adjust image size, resolution, color mode, and make tonal and color corrections.
- **Layer:** Create, manage, and manipulate layers, layer groups, and layer styles.
- **Type:** Add, edit, and format text.
- **Select:** Create, modify, and refine selections.
- **Filter:** Apply a wide range of filters to enhance, stylize, or distort images.
- **3D:** Access Photoshop's 3D features (note that 3D features are being gradually phased out).
- **View:** Control zoom level, screen mode, show/hide guides, grids, and rulers, and manage proofing options.
- **Window:** Show, hide, and arrange panels. Also provides access to different workspaces.
- **Help:** Access online help, tutorials, and information about your Photoshop version.

2.4 The Options Bar: Contextual Tool Settings

The Options Bar is a dynamic element that changes depending on which tool you have selected. It provides quick access to settings and options specific to that tool. For example, if you select the Brush tool, the Options Bar will display options for brush size, hardness, opacity, blending mode, and more.

Get into the habit of glancing at the Options Bar whenever you select a new tool. It's essential for controlling the behavior of the tool and achieving the desired results.

2.5 The Tools Panel: Your Essential Toolkit

The Tools Panel is your primary arsenal for working with images in Photoshop. It contains a wide range of tools, grouped by functionality.

- **Hover for Tool Tips:** Hover your mouse cursor over any tool in the Tools Panel to see its name and a brief description (if Tool Tips are enabled in Preferences).
- **Click and Hold for Hidden Tools:** Many tool icons have a small triangle in the bottom-right corner. This indicates that there are additional, related tools hidden beneath. Click and hold the tool icon to reveal the hidden tools and select the one you need.
- **Keyboard Shortcuts:** Each tool has a keyboard shortcut (displayed in the Tool Tip). Learning these shortcuts can significantly speed up your workflow.
- **Here are some of the most commonly used tool groups:**
- **Move Tool (V):** Moves selections, layers, and guides.
- **Marquee Tools (M):** Make rectangular, elliptical, single-row, or single-column selections.
- **Lasso Tools (L):** Make freehand, polygonal, or magnetic selections.
- **Object Selection Tool, Quick Selection Tool, Magic Wand Tool (W):** These tools use AI or color similarity to help make selections.
- **Crop Tool, Perspective Crop Tool, Slice Tool, Slice Select Tool (C):** Crop and straighten images, correct perspective, and divide images into sections for web optimization.
- **Frame Tool (K):** Creates image placeholders.
- **Eyedropper Tool, 3D Material Eyedropper Tool, Color Sampler Tool, Ruler Tool, Note Tool, Count Tool (I):** Sample colors, measure distances, add notes, and count objects.
- **Spot Healing Brush Tool, Healing Brush Tool, Patch Tool, Content-Aware Move Tool, Red Eye Tool (J):** Retouch and repair images.
- **Brush Tool, Pencil Tool, Color Replacement Tool, Mixer Brush Tool (B):** Paint and draw with various brush tips and settings.
- **Clone Stamp Tool, Pattern Stamp Tool (S):** Clone or paint with a pattern.
- **History Brush Tool, Art History Brush Tool (Y):** Paint with a previous state of the image.
- **Eraser Tool, Background Eraser Tool, Magic Eraser Tool (E):** Erase pixels or make them transparent.
- **Gradient Tool, Paint Bucket Tool, 3D Material Drop Tool (G):** Fill areas with gradients or solid colors.
- **Dodge Tool, Burn Tool, Sponge Tool (O):** Lighten, darken, or adjust the saturation of specific areas.
- **Pen Tool, Freeform Pen Tool, Add Anchor Point Tool, Delete Anchor Point Tool, Convert Point Tool (P):** Create precise vector paths and shapes.
- **Type Tools (T):** Add horizontal and vertical text, as well as text on a path.
- **Path Selection Tool, Direct Selection Tool (A):** Select and manipulate paths and anchor points.

- **Rectangle Tool, Rounded Rectangle Tool, Ellipse Tool, Polygon Tool, Line Tool, Custom Shape Tool (U):** Draw basic geometric shapes and custom shapes.
- **Hand Tool (H):** Pan around the image.
- **Rotate View Tool (R):** Rotate the entire canvas.
- **Zoom Tool (Z):** Zoom in and out of the image.

2.6 Understanding and Managing Panels

Panels are essential for accessing and controlling various aspects of your Photoshop workflow. They provide detailed settings, options, and information related to different functionalities.

2.6.1 Essential Panels: Layers, Adjustments, Properties
While Photoshop has many panels, these three are fundamental:
- **Layers Panel:** Arguably the most important panel in Photoshop. It allows you to manage the different layers that make up your image. You can create, delete, duplicate, hide, show, group, link, arrange, and apply blending modes and opacity to layers.
- **Adjustments Panel:** Provides quick access to non-destructive adjustment layers, which allow you to make tonal and color corrections to your image without permanently altering the original pixel data. Examples include Brightness/Contrast, Levels, Curves, Hue/Saturation, and more.
- **Properties Panel:** A context-sensitive panel that displays settings and options relevant to the currently selected layer or tool. For example, if you select a text layer, the Properties panel will show options for font, size, color, and other text attributes. If you select an adjustment layer, it will show the controls for that specific adjustment.

2.6.2 Customizing Your Panel Layout
Photoshop allows you to customize the arrangement of panels to suit your preferences and workflow:
- **Showing and Hiding Panels:** Go to **Window** in the Menu Bar. A checkmark next to a panel's name indicates that it's currently visible. Click on a panel name to show or hide it.
- **Rearranging Panels:** Click and drag the tab of a panel (the area with the panel's name) to move it to a different location. You can dock panels together, create new panel groups, or let them float freely.
- **2.6.3 Docking, Undocking, and Collapsing Panels**
- **Docking:** Drag a panel tab towards the edge of another panel or panel group until you see a blue highlight appear, then release the mouse button to dock the panel.
- **Undocking:** Click and drag a panel tab away from its docked position to make it a floating panel.
- **Collapsing and Expanding:** Double-click on the tab of a panel group to collapse it into icons, saving screen space. Double-click again to expand it. You

can also click the small double arrows in the top right corner of a panel group to collapse and expand.

2.7 Working with Multiple Documents

Photoshop allows you to have multiple documents open simultaneously. Each document appears in its own tabbed window within the main workspace.

- **Switching Between Documents:** Click on the tab of the document you want to view.
- **Arranging Document Windows:** Go to **Window > Arrange** to choose from various layout options for multiple documents, such as:
    - **Consolidate All to Tabs:** Combines all open documents into a single window with tabs.
    - **Tile:** Arranges the documents in a grid.
    - **Float in Window:** Makes a document a separate, floating window.
    - **Float All in Windows:** Makes all open documents separate, floating windows.

- **Moving Images Between Documents:** You can drag and drop layers or selections from one document window to another.

2.8 Customizing Your Workspace for Efficiency

Once you've become familiar with the various panels and tools, you can start customizing your workspace to create a more efficient and personalized editing environment.

- **Arrange Panels:** Position the panels you use most frequently in easily accessible locations.
- **Create Custom Panel Groups:** Group related panels together to keep your workspace organized.
- **Save Custom Workspaces:** Once you have a panel arrangement you like, you can save it as a custom workspace (see the next section).

2.9 Using Workspaces and Creating Your Own

Photoshop comes with several pre-configured workspaces designed for different tasks (e.g., Essentials, Photography, Painting, Graphic and Web). You can access these workspaces from the **Window > Workspace** menu or by clicking the Workspace switcher icon in the Options Bar (it looks like a small square with a dropdown arrow).

Creating a Custom Workspace:
1. **Arrange your panels and customize the interface to your liking.**
2. **Go to Window > Workspace > New Workspace.**
3. **Give your workspace a descriptive name.**

4. **Choose whether to save Keyboard Shortcuts, Menus, and Tool Bar settings as part of the workspace (recommended).**
5. **Click Save.**

Now you can easily switch to your custom workspace whenever you need it by selecting it from the Workspace menu. You can also delete, reset, or update your custom workspace.

This chapter has provided a thorough introduction to the Photoshop workspace. You've learned about the Menu Bar, Options Bar, Tools Panel, essential panels, and how to manage multiple documents. You've also discovered how to customize your workspace and create your own personalized layouts. As you continue through this book, you'll become increasingly familiar with these elements, and they'll become second nature to you. In the next chapter, we'll delve into the core concepts of working with digital images in Photoshop, including understanding resolution, color modes, and file formats.

Understanding Images and Color

Before you start manipulating images in Photoshop, it's crucial to grasp some fundamental concepts about how digital images are structured and how color is represented. This chapter will explore the difference between raster and vector graphics, explain image resolution and size, delve into common file formats, and introduce you to color modes, bit depth, and color management basics.

3.1 Raster vs. Vector Graphics: What's the Difference?

Digital images generally fall into two main categories: raster and vector. Understanding the distinction between these two types is essential for choosing the right tools and techniques in Photoshop and other graphics applications.

- **Raster Graphics (Bitmap Images):**
    - **Made up of Pixels:** Raster images are composed of a grid of tiny squares called pixels. Each pixel contains color information.
    - **Resolution-Dependent:** The quality of a raster image is dependent on its resolution, which is the number of pixels per inch (PPI). When you enlarge a raster image beyond its original size, it can become pixelated or blurry because the software has to create new pixels based on existing ones.
    - **Best for Photographs and Realistic Images:** Raster graphics are ideal for representing images with continuous tones and subtle gradations of color, such as photographs.
    - **Examples:** JPEG, PNG, GIF, TIFF, PSD (Photoshop's native format)
    - **Photoshop is primarily a raster-based editor.**

- **Vector Graphics:**
    - **Made up of Mathematical Equations:** Vector graphics are defined by mathematical equations that describe lines, curves, and shapes.
    - **Resolution-Independent:** Vector images can be scaled up or down infinitely without losing quality because the software simply recalculates the equations to redraw the image at the new size.
    - **Best for Logos, Illustrations, and Typography:** Vector graphics are ideal for creating artwork that needs to be resized frequently without losing sharpness, such as logos, illustrations, and text.
    - **Examples:** SVG, EPS, AI (Adobe Illustrator's native format)
    - **Photoshop has some vector capabilities (e.g., shape tools, text), but it's not a primary vector editor like Adobe Illustrator.**

In a nutshell: Raster images are like paintings made up of tiny dots, while vector images are like drawings made from precise lines and curves defined by mathematical formulas.

3.2 Image Resolution and Size: Pixels, PPI, and DPI Explained

- **Pixels:** The fundamental building blocks of raster images. Each pixel represents a single color value.
- **Image Size:** Refers to the dimensions of an image, usually expressed in pixels (e.g., 1920 pixels wide by 1080 pixels high).

- **Resolution (PPI):** Pixels Per Inch (PPI) describes the density of pixels in an image. It determines how sharp or detailed an image will appear when printed or displayed on a screen. A higher PPI generally means a sharper image.
  - **Screen Resolution:** For images intended for display on screens (e.g., websites, social media), a resolution of 72 PPI is often considered standard. However, modern high-resolution displays often benefit from higher resolutions.
  - **Print Resolution:** For high-quality printed images, a resolution of 300 PPI is generally recommended.

- **DPI (Dots Per Inch):** DPI refers to the number of ink dots a printer can lay down per inch of paper. While often confused with PPI, DPI is a characteristic of the printer, not the digital image itself. However, a higher image PPI will generally translate to a better-looking print when combined with a high DPI printer.

Important Considerations:

- **Resampling:** When you change the resolution or dimensions of a raster image in Photoshop, you're resampling it. This means you're either adding or removing pixels.
  - **Downsampling:** Reducing the number of pixels. This generally results in a smaller file size but can also lead to a loss of detail.
  - **Upsampling:** Increasing the number of pixels. Photoshop has to interpolate (guess) the color values of the new pixels based on the existing ones. This can lead to a loss of sharpness or pixelation if done excessively. It is generally best to avoid upsampling whenever possible.

- **Image Size Dialog Box:** In Photoshop, you can adjust image size and resolution using the **Image > Image Size** dialog box. Here you can control the dimensions, resolution, and resampling method.

3.3 Common Image File Formats (JPEG, PNG, TIFF, GIF, PSD, etc.)

Different image file formats are suited for different purposes. Here's a rundown of some of the most common formats you'll encounter in Photoshop:

- **JPEG (JPG):**
  - **Lossy Compression:** JPEG uses a compression algorithm that discards some image data to reduce file size. This makes it suitable for web use and sharing,

but it's not ideal for images that require perfect fidelity or will undergo repeated editing.

- **Best for:** Photographs and images with continuous tones intended for web or digital display.

- **PNG:**
  - **Lossless Compression:** PNG uses a compression method that doesn't discard any image data, preserving quality.
  - **Supports Transparency:** PNG supports alpha transparency, allowing you to create images with transparent backgrounds.
  - **Best for:** Web graphics, logos, illustrations, and images that require transparency. There are two main types of PNG files:

  - **PNG-8:** Similar to GIF, supports 256 colors, and is suitable for simple images.
  - **PNG-24:** Supports millions of colors, and is ideal for photographs and complex images that require transparency.

- **GIF:**
  - **Lossless Compression:** Similar to PNG, but limited to 256 colors.
  - **Supports Animation:** GIF is the standard format for creating simple animations for the web.
  - **Best for:** Simple web graphics, small animations, and images with limited color palettes.

- **TIFF (TIF):**
  - **Lossless or Lossy Compression:** TIFF can use either lossless or lossy compression, making it a versatile format.
  - **High Quality:** Often used for archiving and print purposes because it can preserve high image quality.
  - **Supports Layers:** TIFF files can store multiple layers, similar to PSD files.
  - **Best for:** High-quality images intended for print, archiving, or professional workflows.

- **PSD:**
  - **Photoshop Document:** PSD is Photoshop's native file format.
  - **Lossless:** Preserves all image data, including layers, adjustments, masks, and other editing information.
  - **Best for:** Work-in-progress files that you intend to continue editing in Photoshop.

- **PSB:**
  - **Photoshop Big Document:** This is similar to PSD but supports much larger file sizes. Use this when your working file exceeds the limitations of PSD.
- **HEIC/HEIF:**
  - **High-Efficiency Image Format:** This newer format provides better compression than JPEG while maintaining similar image quality.
  - **Used by:** Apple devices (iPhones, iPads) for photos.

- **Note:** You may need a plugin to work with HEIC/HEIF files in older versions of Photoshop. Photoshop 2025 is expected to fully support this format.

Choosing the Right Format: When saving an image, consider the intended use (web, print, archiving), the need for transparency, the desired level of quality, and file size limitations.

3.4 Color Modes: RGB, CMYK, Grayscale, and More

Color modes determine how colors are represented and combined in a digital image. Here are some of the most important color modes in Photoshop:

- **RGB (Red, Green, Blue):**
  - **Additive Color Model:** RGB is an additive color model, meaning that colors are created by adding different intensities of red, green, and blue light.
  - **Used for Screens:** RGB is the standard color mode for images intended for display on screens (monitors, TVs, mobile devices).
  - **Wide Gamut:** RGB can represent a wide range of colors.

- **CMYK (Cyan, Magenta, Yellow, Key/Black):**
  - **Subtractive Color Model:** CMYK is a subtractive color model, meaning that colors are created by subtracting different amounts of cyan, magenta, yellow, and black ink from white.
  - **Used for Print:** CMYK is the standard color mode for printed materials.
  - **Smaller Gamut:** CMYK has a smaller color gamut than RGB, meaning it can't represent all the colors that can be displayed on a screen.

- **Grayscale:**
  - **Uses Shades of Gray:** Grayscale images use only shades of gray, ranging from black to white.
  - **Smaller File Size:** Grayscale images typically have smaller file sizes than color images.

- **Other Color Modes:**
  - **Indexed Color:** Limited to a maximum of 256 colors (like GIF).
  - **Lab Color:** A device-independent color model that represents colors based on human perception. It has a very wide gamut.
  - **Duotone:** Uses two colors to create a vintage or artistic effect.
  - **Multichannel:** Allows you to work with individual color channels, used in advanced printing and color separation workflows.

Converting Color Modes: You can convert an image from one color mode to another in Photoshop (**Image > Mode**), but be aware that some color information may be lost or altered during the conversion, especially when converting from RGB to CMYK.

3.5 Bit Depth: 8-bit, 16-bit, and 32-bit Explained

Bit depth refers to the amount of color information stored for each pixel in an image. Higher bit depths allow for more shades of each color, resulting in smoother gradations and greater detail, especially in highlights and shadows.

- **8-bit:** The most common bit depth. Each color channel (Red, Green, Blue) can have 256 possible values ($2^8 = 256$). This results in a total of 16.7 million possible colors (256 x 256 x 256).
- **16-bit:** Each color channel can have 65,536 possible values ($2^{16} = 65{,}536$). This results in trillions of possible colors. 16-bit images offer significantly more detail and flexibility for editing, especially when making significant tonal adjustments.
- **32-bit:** Primarily used for HDR (High Dynamic Range) images. Each channel can have over 4 billion possible values. 32-bit images contain a vast amount of tonal information, capturing a wider range of brightness levels than what can be displayed on standard monitors or printed.

Benefits of Higher Bit Depth:
- **Smoother Gradations:** Reduces banding or posterization artifacts, especially in areas with subtle tonal changes.
- **Greater Editing Flexibility:** Allows for more extreme adjustments without degrading image quality.
- **More Detail in Highlights and Shadows:** Preserves detail in the brightest and darkest areas of the image.

Trade-offs:
- **Larger File Size:** Higher bit depth images have significantly larger file sizes.
- **Increased Processing Demands:** Working with 16-bit and 32-bit images can be more demanding on your computer's resources.

When to Use Higher Bit Depth:
- **High-Quality Images:** When image quality is paramount, such as for professional photography or print.
- **Extensive Editing:** When you plan to make significant tonal adjustments or work with HDR images.

3.6 Color Profiles and Color Management Basics

Color management is a complex topic, but understanding the basics is essential for ensuring accurate and consistent color reproduction across different devices (monitors, printers, etc.).

- **Color Profiles:** A color profile is a set of data that describes the color characteristics of a particular device or color space. It defines how colors should be interpreted and displayed.
    - **Common Color Profiles:**
- **sRGB:** A standard color profile for web and digital display.
    - **Adobe RGB (1998):** A wider-gamut color profile often used in professional photography and print.
    - **ProPhoto RGB:** An even wider-gamut color profile used for high-end image editing.
    - **Device-Specific Profiles:** Profiles created specifically for your monitor, printer, or scanner.
    - **Embedding Color Profiles:** When you save an image in Photoshop, you can choose to embed a color profile. This ensures that the color information is interpreted correctly when the image is opened on other devices or in other applications.
    - **Color Settings:** Photoshop's Color Settings (**Edit > Color Settings**) allow you to define your working color spaces, color management policies, and conversion options.

Basic Color Management Workflow:

1. **Calibrate Your Monitor:** Use a hardware calibration device to ensure that your monitor is displaying colors accurately.
2. **Choose a Working Color Space:** Select an appropriate color space for your project (e.g., sRGB for web, Adobe RGB for print).
3. **Assign or Convert Color Profiles:** Make sure your images have the correct color profiles assigned or convert them if necessary.
4. **Soft Proofing:** Use Photoshop's soft proofing features (**View > Proof Setup**) to preview how your image will look when printed or displayed on a different device.

3.7 Introduction to Photoshop Generative AI Features

Photoshop 2025 includes a suite of features that leverage the power of generative artificial intelligence. These tools can assist with various tasks, including:

- **Content-Aware Fill:** Intelligently fills in selected areas of an image by analyzing the surrounding content.
- **Neural Filters:** Apply a wide range of creative and restorative effects powered by AI, such as skin smoothing, style transfer, and colorization.
- **Object Selection Tool:** Automatically detects and selects objects in an image with remarkable accuracy.
- **Generative Expand:** Allows users to expand an image's canvas and use a prompt to generate new content to fill the space.
- **Generative Fill:** Allows users to remove or add objects to an image using AI.

Key Considerations for Generative AI:

- **Ethical Use:** Be mindful of the ethical implications of using AI to manipulate images.
- **Artistic Control:** While AI can be a powerful tool, it's important to maintain artistic control over your work. Use AI as a starting point and refine the results manually as needed.
- **Experimentation:** Don't be afraid to experiment with different settings and prompts to discover the full potential of these tools.

This chapter has laid the groundwork for understanding digital images and color in Photoshop. You've learned about raster and vector graphics, resolution, file formats, color modes, bit depth, and the basics of color management. You've also been introduced to the exciting possibilities of Photoshop's Generative AI features. In the next chapter, we'll move on to creating and importing documents, putting this foundational knowledge into practice!

Mastering Layers

Layers are the cornerstone of non-destructive editing in Photoshop. They allow you to work on different elements of your image independently, without permanently altering the original pixels. Think of layers like transparent sheets of acetate stacked on top of each other. You can draw, paint, or place images on each sheet, and then rearrange, edit, and blend them to create a composite image. This chapter will teach you everything you need to know about using layers effectively, from the basics to advanced techniques.

4.1 What are Layers and Why are They Important?

Imagine you're painting a landscape. Instead of painting directly onto a single canvas, you decide to paint the sky on one transparent sheet, the mountains on another, and the trees on a third. This is essentially how layers work in Photoshop.

Benefits of Using Layers:

- **Non-Destructive Editing:** Changes you make to one layer don't affect the other layers. This allows you to experiment freely, make revisions easily, and preserve the original image data.
- **Flexibility and Control:** You can adjust the position, opacity, blending mode, and other properties of each layer independently, giving you fine-grained control over the final image.
- **Organization:** Layers help you keep your projects organized by separating different elements into logical units.
- **Compositing:** Layers are essential for creating composite images, where you combine elements from multiple sources into a single image.

Types of Layers:

Photoshop offers various types of layers, each designed for a specific purpose:

- **Pixel Layers (Raster Layers):** The most common type of layer. They contain pixel data and are used for painting, retouching, and manipulating images.
- **Adjustment Layers:** Apply non-destructive tonal and color adjustments to the layers below them. Examples include Brightness/Contrast, Levels, Curves, and Hue/Saturation.
- **Type Layers:** Contain editable text.
- **Shape Layers:** Contain vector shapes created with the shape tools.
- **Smart Objects:** Special layers that preserve the original image data and allow for non-destructive transformations and filtering.
- **Fill Layers:** These apply a solid color, gradient, or pattern to the layer.
- **Video Layers:** Used for working with video clips.

4.2 The Layers Panel: Your Layer Control Center

The Layers Panel is your primary interface for working with layers. To show or hide the Layers Panel, go to **Window > Layers** (or press **F7**).

Key Components of the Layers Panel:

- **Layer Thumbnails:** Small previews of the contents of each layer.
- **Layer Names:** Descriptive names for each layer. Double-click a layer name to edit it.
- **Visibility Icon (Eye):** Click the eye icon to show or hide a layer.
- **Layer Blending Mode:** A drop-down menu that controls how a layer blends with the layers below it.
- **Layer Opacity:** A slider that controls the transparency of a layer.
- **Fill:** Similar to Opacity but affects only the pixels on the layer, not layer styles.
- **Lock Options:** Various options for locking layers to prevent accidental changes.
- **Add Layer Mask:** Adds a layer mask to the selected layer.
- **Add Layer Style:** Applies layer styles like drop shadows, glows, and bevels.
- **Create New Fill or Adjustment Layer:** Adds a new fill or adjustment layer.
- **Create a New Group:** Creates a new layer group for organizing layers.
- **Create a New Layer:** Adds a new blank pixel layer.
- **Delete Layer:** Deletes the selected layer or layer group.
- **Panel Menu:** Provides access to additional layer-related commands and options.
- **Filtering Options:** This section provides tools for filtering the view of the layers panel based on specific criteria.

4.3 Creating, Duplicating, and Deleting Layers

- **Creating a New Layer:**
  - Click the **Create a New Layer** button at the bottom of the Layers Panel.
  - Go to **Layer > New > Layer**.
  - Use the keyboard shortcut **Shift+Ctrl+N** (Windows) or **Shift+Cmd+N** (macOS).
  - **Duplicating a Layer:**
  - Drag the layer you want to duplicate onto the **Create a New Layer** button.
  - Right-click (Windows) or Ctrl-click (macOS) on the layer and choose **Duplicate Layer**.
  - Go to **Layer > Duplicate Layer**.
  - Use the keyboard shortcut **Ctrl+J** (Windows) or **Cmd+J** (macOS).

- **Deleting a Layer:**
  - Click the **Delete Layer** button at the bottom of the Layers Panel.
  - Drag the layer you want to delete onto the **Delete Layer** button.
  - Right-click (Windows) or Ctrl-click (macOS) on the layer and choose **Delete Layer**.

- Select the layer and press the **Delete** key.

4.4 Naming and Organizing Layers with Groups

As your projects become more complex, keeping your layers organized is crucial.

- **Naming Layers:** Double-click on a layer name in the Layers Panel to edit it. Choose descriptive names that clearly indicate the contents of each layer (e.g., "Background," "Sky," "Portrait," "Text").

- **Creating Layer Groups:**
    - Click the **Create a New Group** button at the bottom of the Layers Panel.
    - Select multiple layers, then right-click (Windows) or Ctrl-click (macOS) and choose **Group from Layers**.
        - Go to **Layer > Group Layers**.
        - Use the keyboard shortcut **Ctrl+G** (Windows) or **Cmd+G** (macOS).

- **Moving Layers into Groups:** Click and drag a layer onto a group's folder icon in the Layers Panel. You can also drag and drop layers between groups.
- **Collapsing and Expanding Groups:** Click the small triangle next to a group's folder icon to collapse or expand it.
- **Color-Coding Layers and Groups:** Right-click (Windows) or Ctrl-click (macOS) on a layer or group and choose a color from the context menu. This can help you visually identify related layers.

4.5 Layer Blending Modes: Creating Unique Effects

Blending modes determine how a layer interacts with the layers beneath it. They offer a wide range of creative possibilities for combining and blending images.

- **Accessing Blending Modes:** In the Layers Panel, select a layer and choose a blending mode from the drop-down menu (it usually says "Normal" by default).
- **Experimentation is Key:** The best way to understand blending modes is to experiment with them. Try different modes and see how they affect your image.

- **Common Blending Modes:**
    - **Normal:** No blending; the layer simply covers the layers below it (subject to its opacity).
    - **Dissolve:** Creates a random, grainy blend.
    - **Darken:** Compares each channel of the active layer to the underlying layer and displays the darker of the two.
    - **Multiply:** Multiplies the colors of the blending layer with the colors of the underlying layers, resulting in a darker image. Often used for creating shadows.
    - **Color Burn:** Darkens the underlying layers based on the colors of the blending layer.

- **Linear Burn:** Darkens the colors, similar to Multiply, but with increased contrast.
- **Darker Color:** Similar to Darken but works on the composite of all channels, not each individually.
- **Lighten:** Compares each channel of the active layer to the underlying layer and displays the lighter of the two.
- **Screen:** Inverts the colors of both layers, multiplies them, and then inverts the result. This creates a lighter image, often used for creating highlights or lightening effects.
- **Color Dodge:** Lightens the underlying layers based on the colors of the blending layer.
- **Linear Dodge (Add):** Similar to Screen, but with increased brightness.
- **Lighter Color:** Similar to Lighten but works on the composite of all channels, not each individually.
- **Overlay:** A combination of Multiply and Screen. It multiplies the dark areas and screens the light areas, increasing contrast and saturation. Often used for dodging and burning.
- **Soft Light:** Similar to Overlay but with a gentler effect.
- **Hard Light:** Creates a more intense effect, similar to shining a harsh spotlight on the image.
- **Vivid Light:** Combines Color Dodge and Color Burn to create a high-contrast effect.
- **Linear Light:** Combines Linear Dodge and Linear Burn to create a high-contrast effect.
- **Pin Light:** Combines Darken and Lighten to create a posterized effect.
- **Hard Mix:** Reduces colors to their primary components based on the blend mode.
- **Difference:** Subtracts the darker color from the lighter color, creating an inverted effect.
- **Exclusion:** Similar to Difference but with lower contrast.
- **Subtract:** Subtracts the pixel values of the blend layer from those of the underlying layers.
- **Divide:** Divides the pixel values of the underlying layers by those of the blend layer.
- **Hue:** Applies the hue of the blending layer to the underlying layers while preserving their luminosity and saturation.
- **Saturation:** Applies the saturation of the blending layer to the underlying layers while preserving their hue and luminosity.
- **Color:** Applies the hue and saturation of the blending layer to the underlying layers while preserving their luminosity. Often used for colorizing images.
- **Luminosity:** Applies the luminosity of the blending layer to the underlying layers while preserving their hue and saturation.

- **Categories of Blending Modes:** The blending modes are grouped into categories in the drop-down menu based on their general effect:
  - **Normal:** Normal, Dissolve
  - **Darken:** Darken, Multiply, Color Burn, Linear Burn, Darker Color

- **Lighten:** Lighten, Screen, Color Dodge, Linear Dodge (Add), Lighter Color
- **Contrast:** Overlay, Soft Light, Hard Light, Vivid Light, Linear Light, Pin Light, Hard Mix
- **Inversion:** Difference, Exclusion[1]
- **Component:** Hue, Saturation, Color, Luminosity

4.6 Layer Opacity and Fill: Controlling Transparency

Opacity and Fill both control the transparency of a layer, but they have subtle differences:

- **Opacity:**
  - **Controls the overall transparency of a layer, including its contents and any applied layer styles.**
  - A value of 100% means the layer is fully opaque.
  - A value of 0% means the layer is completely transparent.

- **Fill:**
  - **Controls the transparency of the layer's contents (pixels) but *not* the layer styles.**
  - This means you can reduce the Fill to 0% to make the pixels on a layer invisible while still keeping any applied layer styles (like drop shadows or glows) fully visible.
  - **Example:** If you have a text layer with a drop shadow and you reduce the Opacity, both the text and the shadow will become more transparent. If you reduce the Fill, only the text will become more transparent, while the drop shadow will remain fully opaque.

4.7 Layer Styles: Adding Depth and Dimension

Layer Styles are non-destructive effects that you can apply to a layer to add visual interest and enhance its appearance. They can create a wide range of effects, from simple drop shadows and glows to more complex bevels and textures.

Applying Layer Styles:
1. **Select the layer** you want to apply a style to in the Layers Panel.
2. **Click the "fx" icon** at the bottom of the Layers Panel (Add a Layer Style).
3. **Choose a style** from the drop-down menu.
4. **Adjust the settings** in the Layer Style dialog box to customize the effect.

Common Layer Styles:
- **Drop Shadow:** Adds a shadow behind the layer's contents.
- **Inner Shadow:** Adds a shadow inside the layer's contents.
- **Outer Glow:** Creates a glow effect around the outside of the layer.
- **Inner Glow:** Creates a glow effect on the inside of the layer.

- **Bevel and Emboss:** Adds a 3D beveled or embossed effect to the layer.
- **Satin:** Applies a smooth, satiny finish.
- **Color Overlay:** Fills the layer with a solid color.
- **Gradient Overlay:** Fills the layer with a gradient.
- **Pattern Overlay:** Fills the layer with a pattern.
- **Stroke:** Adds an outline around the layer.

Layer Style Dialog Box:

The Layer Style dialog box is where you fine-tune the settings for each style. It has a list of styles on the left and options for the selected style on the right.

- **Blending Options:** The top section of the Layer Style dialog. This section is always available, even if no specific style is selected. It allows you to adjust the general blending options of the layer, including Advanced Blending settings.
- **Structure:** Many styles, such as Bevel and Emboss and Drop Shadow, have settings related to their basic structure, such as Size, Depth, and Angle.
- **Shading:** Some styles also have settings that control the shading of the effect, such as Altitude, Gloss Contour, and Highlight/Shadow Mode.
- **Preview:** Make sure the "Preview" checkbox is checked so you can see the effects in real time as you adjust the settings.

Managing Layer Styles:

- **Copying and Pasting Layer Styles:** Right-click (Windows) or Control-click (macOS) on a layer with styles and choose "Copy Layer Style." Then, right-click on another layer and choose "Paste Layer Style."
- **Editing Layer Styles:** Double-click the "fx" icon next to a layer's name in the Layers Panel to reopen the Layer Style dialog box and make changes.
- **Showing and Hiding Layer Styles:** Click the small triangle next to the "fx" icon to expand or collapse the list of applied styles. Click the eye icon next to a style to show or hide it.
- **Clearing Layer Styles:** Right-click on a layer with styles and choose "Clear Layer Style" to remove all styles from the layer.

4.8 Clipping Masks: Confining Effects to Specific Layers

Clipping masks are a powerful way to restrict the visibility of one layer (or multiple layers) to the shape or transparency of another layer (the base layer). In essence, the base layer acts as a "mask" for the clipped layers.

Creating a Clipping Mask:

1. **Arrange the layers:** Place the layer(s) you want to clip *above* the base layer in the Layers Panel.
2. **Create the clipping mask:**
   - **Option 1 (Menu):** Select the layer(s) you want to clip, then go to **Layer > Create Clipping Mask**.
   - **Option 2 (Alt/Option-Click):** Hold down **Alt** (Windows) or **Option** (macOS) and click on the line *between* the two layers in the Layers Panel.
   - **Option 3 (Right-Click):** Right-click (Windows) or Control-click (macOS) on the layer you want to clip and choose **Create Clipping Mask**.
   - **Visual Indicator:** In the Layers Panel, a clipped layer is indented and has a small downward-pointing arrow pointing to the base layer below it.
   - **Example:** You have a photo of a texture and a text layer. If you clip the texture layer to the text layer, the texture will only be visible *within* the shape of the text.

Releasing a Clipping Mask:

- **Option 1 (Menu):** Select the clipped layer, then go to **Layer > Release Clipping Mask**.
- **Option 2 (Alt/Option-Click):** Hold down **Alt** (Windows) or **Option** (macOS) and click on the line between the clipped layer and the base layer.
- **Option 3 (Right-Click):** Right-click (Windows) or Control-click (macOS) on the clipped layer and choose **Release Clipping Mask**.

4.9 Layer Masks: Non-Destructive Editing

Layer masks are one of the most essential tools for non-destructive editing in Photoshop. They allow you to hide or reveal portions of a layer without permanently erasing any pixels.

How Layer Masks Work:

- **Grayscale Mask:** A layer mask is essentially a grayscale image associated with a layer.
- **White Reveals, Black Conceals:** White areas on the mask reveal the corresponding parts of the layer, while black areas conceal them. Shades of gray create varying levels of transparency.

Creating a Layer Mask:

1. **Select the layer** you want to add a mask to.
2. **Click the "Add layer mask" button** at the bottom of the Layers Panel (it looks like a rectangle with a circle inside).

Editing a Layer Mask:

1. **Select the mask thumbnail:** In the Layers Panel, click on the mask thumbnail (the white rectangle) next to the layer thumbnail. You'll see a double border around the mask thumbnail, indicating that it's active.

2. **Paint on the mask:**
   - Use the **Brush tool** with **black** to hide portions of the layer.
   - Use the **Brush tool** with **white** to reveal portions of the layer.
   - Use shades of **gray** to create partial transparency.
3. **Other Tools:** You can also use other tools like the **Gradient tool**, **selection tools**, or even **filters** on a layer mask to create more complex masking effects.

Disabling/Enabling a Layer Mask:

- **Shift-click** on the mask thumbnail to temporarily disable the mask. A red "X" will appear over the thumbnail. Shift-click again to re-enable it.

Deleting a Layer Mask:

- **Drag the mask thumbnail** to the **Delete Layer** button at the bottom of the Layers Panel.
- **Right-click** (Windows) or **Control-click** (macOS) on the mask thumbnail and choose **Delete Layer Mask**.

Applying a Layer Mask:

- **Right-click** on the mask thumbnail and choose **Apply Layer Mask**. This permanently applies the mask to the layer, removing the hidden pixels.

4.10 Smart Objects: Preserving Image Quality

Smart Objects are special layers that contain image data from raster or vector images. They offer several advantages for non-destructive editing:

- **Non-Destructive Transformations:** You can scale, rotate, skew, distort, or apply perspective to a Smart Object without losing original image data. You can always revert to the original state.
- **Non-Destructive Filters:** Filters applied to Smart Objects are called Smart Filters. They remain editable, allowing you to change the filter settings at any time.
- **Linked Smart Objects:** You can create linked Smart Objects that are connected to an external file. When you update the external file, all instances of the linked Smart Object in your Photoshop document are automatically updated. This is particularly useful when working with logos or other elements that are used multiple times in a design.
- **Embedded Smart Objects:** You can also embed external files as Smart Objects. These are self-contained and not linked to the original file.

Creating Smart Objects:

- **From Existing Layers:** Right-click (Windows) or Control-click (macOS) on a layer or group of layers and choose **Convert to Smart Object**.
- **Placing Files as Smart Objects:** Go to **File > Place Embedded** or **File > Place Linked** to place an image as a Smart Object.
- **Editing Smart Objects:**
- **Double-click the Smart Object thumbnail** in the Layers Panel. This will open the Smart Object in a new document window where you can edit its contents. Save the changes, and the Smart Object will update in your main document.

Rasterizing Smart Objects:

- **Right-click** on the Smart Object layer and choose **Rasterize Layer**. This converts the Smart Object into a regular pixel layer. **Note:** Once you rasterize a Smart Object, you lose the benefits of non-destructive editing.

4.11 Introduction to AI-Powered Layer Management

Photoshop 2025 is expected to introduce more AI-powered features to streamline layer management. While specific details might not be available until the official release, here are some potential areas where AI could play a role:

- **Automatic Layer Grouping:** AI could analyze the contents of your layers and automatically group related elements together, making it easier to organize complex projects.
- **Intelligent Layer Naming:** Photoshop could suggest more descriptive names for layers based on their content, saving you time and effort. You could also pre-define naming conventions that Photoshop could follow.
- **Smart Layer Selection:** AI could help you quickly select specific layers based on their content, even in complex documents with many layers. Imagine selecting all layers containing "text," "people," or "background elements" with a single click.

- **Context-Aware Layer Suggestions:** As you work, Photoshop could suggest relevant layers or actions based on your current task. For instance, if you're retouching a portrait, it might suggest creating a new layer for dodging and burning.
- **AI-Assisted Masking:** AI could help refine layer masks, especially around complex edges like hair or fur.

This concludes Chapter 4! You've now mastered the fundamentals of working with layers in Photoshop. You've learned about layer types, the Layers Panel, blending modes, layer opacity, layer styles, clipping masks, layer masks, and Smart Objects. You're well-equipped to tackle more advanced editing techniques and create complex composite images. In the

next chapter, we'll explore selections and masking in greater depth, building on the foundation you've established here.

Selections and Masking

The ability to make precise selections is fundamental to mastering Photoshop. Selections allow you to isolate specific areas of an image so that you can apply edits, adjustments, or effects to those areas only. Whether you want to remove a background, change the color of an object, or combine elements from different images, selections are the key.

This chapter will cover a variety of selection tools, from the basic Marquee and Lasso tools to the more advanced, AI-powered Object Selection tool. We'll also explore the Select and Mask workspace, which provides a dedicated environment for refining selections and creating masks.

5.1 The Importance of Accurate Selections

Why are accurate selections so important? Here are a few key reasons:

- **Precise Edits:** Selections allow you to target your edits precisely where you want them. You can adjust the color, tone, or sharpness of a specific object without affecting the rest of the image.
- **Seamless Compositing:** When combining elements from different images, accurate selections are crucial for creating a believable composite. Jagged or inaccurate selections will make the composite look artificial.
- **Non-Destructive Workflow:** Selections, especially when combined with layer masks, enable a non-destructive workflow. You can always go back and refine your selections without permanently altering the original image data.
- **Efficiency:** Making accurate selections from the outset saves you time and effort in the long run. You'll spend less time cleaning up messy edges or redoing your work.

5.2 Marquee Tools: Rectangular, Elliptical, Single Row, Single Column

The Marquee tools are the simplest selection tools in Photoshop. They allow you to create basic geometric selections.

- **Rectangular Marquee Tool (M):** Creates rectangular selections.
- **Modifier Keys:**
    - **Shift:** Constrains the selection to a perfect square.
    - **Alt (Windows) / Option (macOS):** Draws the selection from the center outward.
    - **Shift+Alt / Shift+Option:** Draws a perfect square from the center.

- **Elliptical Marquee Tool (M):** Creates elliptical selections.
- **Modifier Keys:**
    - **Shift:** Constrains the selection to a perfect circle.
    - **Alt (Windows) / Option (macOS):** Draws the selection from the center outward.
    - **Shift+Alt / Shift+Option:** Draws a perfect circle from the center.

- **Single Row Marquee Tool:** Creates a selection that is one pixel high and spans the entire width of the image.
- **Single Column Marquee Tool:** Creates a selection that is one pixel wide and spans the entire height of the image.

Making Selections with the Marquee Tools:

1. **Select the desired Marquee tool** from the Tools Panel.
2. **Click and drag** in the document window to create the selection.
3. **Use modifier keys** (Shift, Alt/Option) to constrain the shape or draw from the center.
4. **Repositioning a Selection:** While making a selection, hold down the **Spacebar** to temporarily turn your cursor into a hand. You can then move your selection and continue making it afterward.

Options Bar Settings for Marquee Tools:

- **New Selection:** Creates a new selection.
- **Add to Selection:** Adds to the existing selection. You can also hold down **Shift** while drawing to add to a selection.
- **Subtract from Selection:** Subtracts from the existing selection. You can also hold down **Alt (Windows) / Option (macOS)** while drawing to subtract from a selection.
- **Intersect with Selection:** Creates a selection from the overlapping area of the new selection and the existing selection. You can also hold down **Shift+Alt / Shift+Option** to intersect.
- **Feather:** Softens the edges of the selection by creating a transition zone. A higher feather value creates a softer, more gradual transition.
- **Anti-alias:** Smooths the edges of the selection by partially filling in pixels along the edge. This option is only available for the Elliptical Marquee Tool.

Style:

- **Normal:** Allows you to freely drag to create the selection.
- **Fixed Aspect Ratio:** Constrains the selection to a specific aspect ratio (e.g., 1:1 for a square, 4:3, 16:9).
- **Fixed Size:** Creates a selection of a specific pixel dimension.

5.3 Lasso Tools: Freehand, Polygonal, and Magnetic

The Lasso tools offer more flexibility than the Marquee tools, allowing you to create freeform selections.

- **Lasso Tool (L):** Creates freehand selections. You simply click and drag to draw the selection outline.
  - **Best for:** Quick, rough selections where precision is not critical.

- **Polygonal Lasso Tool (L):** Creates selections made up of straight-line segments. You click to place anchor points, and Photoshop connects them with straight lines.
  - **Best for:** Selecting objects with straight edges or polygonal shapes.
  - **Closing the Selection:** Double-click, press **Enter/Return**, or click on the starting point to close the selection.

- **Magnetic Lasso Tool (L):** "Snaps" to edges as you trace around an object. It detects edges based on contrast and color differences.
  - **Best for:** Selecting objects with well-defined edges against a contrasting background.
  - **Adjusting on the Fly:** Press **[** or **]** to decrease or increase the detection width.
  - **Adding Points Manually:** Click to add anchor points manually if the tool is not snapping correctly.

Options Bar Settings for Lasso Tools:

- **New Selection, Add to Selection, Subtract from Selection, Intersect with Selection:** Same as the Marquee tools.
- **Feather:** Same as the Marquee tools.
- **Anti-alias:** Same as the Marquee tools.
- **Width (Magnetic Lasso):** Sets the detection width, which is the area around the cursor where the tool looks for edges.
- **Contrast (Magnetic Lasso):** Sets the tool's sensitivity to edges. A higher contrast value is useful for well-defined edges, while a lower value is better for softer edges.
- **Frequency (Magnetic Lasso):** Determines how often the tool places anchor points. A higher frequency creates a more precise selection.

5.4 Quick Selection Tool and Magic Wand Tool

These tools make selections based on color and tonal similarities.

- **Quick Selection Tool (W):** You "paint" over an area, and the tool automatically expands the selection to include similar pixels.
  - **Best for:** Quickly selecting objects or areas with relatively uniform colors and well-defined edges.
  - **Brush Size:** Adjust the brush size using the **[** and **]** keys. A larger brush covers more area, while a smaller brush is more precise.
  - **Adding and Subtracting:** Use the **Add to Selection** and **Subtract from Selection** options in the Options Bar or hold down **Shift** (add) or **Alt/Option** (subtract) while painting.

- **Magic Wand Tool (W):** Selects pixels based on their color similarity to the pixel you click.
  - **Best for:** Selecting areas with solid colors or smooth gradients, such as a clear blue sky.
  - **Tolerance:** A crucial setting that determines the range of colors that will be selected. A lower tolerance selects a narrower range of colors, while a higher tolerance selects a wider range.
  - **Contiguous:** When checked, the tool only selects adjacent pixels that fall within the tolerance range. When unchecked, it selects all pixels in the image that meet the criteria, even if they are not connected.
  - **Sample All Layers:** When checked, the tool considers pixels from all visible layers when making the selection. When unchecked, it only samples from the currently active layer.

Options Bar Settings:
- **New Selection, Add to Selection, Subtract from Selection, Intersect with Selection:** Same as the Marquee and Lasso tools.
- **Sample Size (Quick Selection Tool):** Point Sample will select based on the color of the single pixel you click on. Other options allow you to sample the average color of the surrounding pixels, which can produce better results.
- **Sample All Layers:** Same as the Magic Wand Tool.

- **Enhance Edge (Quick Selection Tool):** This option can help to smooth and refine the selection edge.

5.5 Object Selection Tool: Harnessing AI for Selection

The Object Selection Tool, introduced in recent versions of Photoshop, leverages the power of Adobe Sensei AI to automatically detect and select objects within an image.

- **How it Works:** The tool analyzes the image and attempts to identify distinct objects based on their shape, color, and texture.
- **Modes:**
  - **Rectangle:** Drag a rectangular marquee around the object you want to select.
  - **Lasso:** Draw a loose lasso around the object.

- **Object Finder:** When this is enabled, Photoshop will automatically highlight potential objects as you hover over them. You can then click on an object to select it.
- **Subtract from Selection:** This allows you to refine the selection by removing unwanted areas.
- **Sample All Layers:** The tool can also take into account multiple layers in its analysis.
- **Object Subtract:** This is particularly useful for cutting out objects.
- **Refine Hair:** This option can help to improve selections around difficult areas like hair and fur.
- **Best for:** Quickly selecting well-defined objects, especially when they are distinct from the background.

5.6 Select Subject and Select and Mask Workspace

These features provide powerful tools for making and refining selections, especially for complex subjects like people or objects with intricate details.

- **Select Subject:**
  - **How it Works:** Uses AI to automatically detect and select the main subject in an image.
- **Accessing it:**
  - Click the **Select Subject** button in the Options Bar when any selection tool is active.
  - Go to **Select > Subject**.
  - **Best for:** Portraits, images with a clear subject against a less prominent background.

- **Select and Mask Workspace:**
  - **Purpose:** A dedicated workspace for refining selections and creating masks. It provides specialized tools and views for fine-tuning edges, dealing with tricky areas like hair and fur, and previewing the selection against different backgrounds.
- **Accessing it:**
  - Click the **Select and Mask** button in the Options Bar when any selection tool is active.
  - Go to **Select > Select and Mask**.
- **Key Tools and Features:**

- **View Modes:** Allows you to preview your selection in various ways (e.g., Onion Skin, Marching Ants, Overlay, On Black, On White, Black & White, On Layers). This allows for easier adjustments.
- **Refine Edge Brush Tool:** Use this tool to paint over soft or complex edges (like hair or fur) to improve the selection.
- **Brush Tool:** Allows you to manually add to or subtract from the selection.
- **Edge Detection:** The Radius slider can help to refine the selection edge by expanding or contracting the area where Photoshop looks for edges. Smart Radius allows Photoshop to vary this radius as needed.
- **Global Refinements:** These settings include options like Smooth, Feather, Contrast, and Shift Edge, which allow for overall adjustments to the selection edge.
- **Output Settings:** Choose how you want to output the refined selection: as a selection, a layer mask, a new layer, a new layer with a layer mask, a new document, or a new document with a layer mask.

Tips for Using Select and Mask:

- **Start with a Good Initial Selection:** Use the Object Selection Tool, Quick Selection Tool, or Select Subject to create a reasonably accurate initial selection before entering the Select and Mask workspace.
- **Use Different View Modes:** Cycle through the different view modes to get a better sense of how your selection looks against various backgrounds.
- **Zoom In and Work on Details:** Use the Zoom Tool (Z) and Hand Tool (H) to navigate around the image and work on the details of the selection edge.
- **Refine Gradually:** Make small, incremental adjustments rather than trying to do everything at once.

5.7 Refining Selections with the Refine Edge Brush

The Refine Edge Brush Tool is a specialized tool within the **Select and Mask** workspace that's particularly useful for improving selections around soft or complex edges, such as hair, fur, or foliage.

How to Use the Refine Edge Brush:

1. **Make an initial selection** using any of the selection tools (Object Selection, Quick Selection, etc.).
2. **Enter the Select and Mask workspace** by clicking the **Select and Mask** button in the Options Bar.
3. **Select the Refine Edge Brush Tool** from the toolbar on the left side of the Select and Mask workspace. It's the second tool from the top.
4. **Adjust the brush size** using the [and] keys.
5. **Paint over the edges** of your selection where you want to refine the transition between the selected and unselected areas. Focus on areas with fine details or soft edges.
6. **Use the various View Modes** (Onion Skin, Marching Ants, Overlay, etc.) to preview the selection against different backgrounds and assess the refinement.
7. **Adjust the Edge Detection and Global Refinements settings** in the Properties panel on the right as needed.

Tips for Using the Refine Edge Brush:
- **Use a smaller brush size** for intricate details.
- **Zoom in** to see the edges more clearly.
- **Don't overdo it.** It's easy to over-refine the edges, which can make them look artificial. Start with subtle adjustments and gradually increase the refinement if necessary.
- **Use the "Show Edge" option** in the View Mode settings to visualize the area that Photoshop is analyzing for edge refinement.
- **Combine with other tools:** You can use the regular Brush tool within Select and Mask to manually add or subtract from the selection, in conjunction with the Refine Edge Brush.

5.8 Saving and Loading Selections

Photoshop allows you to save selections so you can reuse them later. This is particularly useful for complex selections that you've spent time refining.

Saving Selections:
1. **Make the selection** you want to save.
2. **Go to Select > Save Selection.**
3. **In the Save Selection dialog box:**
   - Give the selection a descriptive name.
   - Choose whether to save it as a new channel or add it to an existing channel.
   - Click **OK**.

Where are Selections Saved?
Selections are saved as alpha channels, which are grayscale channels that store selection information. You can view them in the **Channels Panel (Window > Channels)**.

Loading Selections:
1. **Go to Select > Load Selection.**
2. **In the Load Selection dialog box:**
   - Choose the saved selection from the **Channel** drop-down menu.
   - Choose an operation (New Selection, Add to Selection, Subtract from Selection, Intersect with Selection).
   - Check the **Invert** option if you want to select the inverse of the saved selection.
   - Click **OK**.

Alternative Ways to Load Selections:
- **From the Channels Panel:**

- **Ctrl-click (Windows) or Cmd-click (macOS)** on the alpha channel thumbnail to load it as a new selection.
- **Ctrl+Alt+Click (Windows) / Cmd+Option+Click (macOS):** Add to current selection.
- **Ctrl+Shift+Click (Windows) / Cmd+Shift+Click (macOS):** Subtract from current selection.
- **Ctrl+Alt+Shift+Click (Windows) / Cmd+Option+Shift+Click (macOS):** Intersect with current selection.
- **Drag and Drop:** Drag the alpha channel thumbnail from the Channels Panel onto the document window to load it as a selection.

5.9 Creating and Editing Layer Masks

Layer masks, as we introduced in Chapter 4, are a powerful way to non-destructively hide or reveal parts of a layer. They are intimately connected with selections because you often use selections to create or refine layer masks.

Creating a Layer Mask from a Selection:
1. **Make a selection** using any of the selection tools.
2. **Select the layer** you want to add a mask to in the Layers Panel.
3. **Click the "Add layer mask" button** at the bottom of the Layers Panel.

What Happens:
- The selected area will remain visible on the layer.
- The unselected area will be hidden (masked out).
- A layer mask thumbnail will appear next to the layer thumbnail in the Layers Panel.

Editing a Layer Mask:
1. **Click on the layer mask thumbnail** in the Layers Panel to make it active.
2. **Paint on the mask with:**
   - **Black:** To hide parts of the layer.
   - **White:** To reveal parts of the layer.
   - **Grays:** To create semi-transparency.
3. You can also use other tools like gradients, selections, and filters on a layer mask.

5.10 Vector Masks: For Precision Edits

Vector masks are similar to layer masks but instead of using pixels, they use vector paths (like those created with the Pen tool) to define the visible and hidden areas of a layer.

Advantages of Vector Masks:
- **Resolution-Independent:** Vector masks can be scaled without losing quality.
- **Precise Edges:** They create crisp, clean edges, making them ideal for masking objects with sharp lines or geometric shapes.
- **Editable Paths:** You can edit the vector paths at any time using the Pen tool and Direct Selection tool.

Creating a Vector Mask:
1. **Select the layer** you want to add a mask to.
2. **Create a path** using the Pen tool or any of the shape tools.
3. **Go to Layer > Vector Mask > Current Path.**

Editing a Vector Mask:

- Use the **Pen tool** and its related tools (Add Anchor Point, Delete Anchor Point, Convert Point) to modify the path.
- Use the **Direct Selection tool** to select and move individual anchor points or path segments.

5.11 Advanced Masking Techniques

Here are a few more advanced masking techniques to expand your creative toolkit:

- **Using Calculations for Masking:** The **Calculations** command (**Image > Calculations**) allows you to blend channels from different layers or from the same layer to create complex masks based on luminosity, color, or other criteria. This is an advanced technique that requires a good understanding of channels.
- **Intersecting Masks:** You can intersect a layer mask with a selection to refine it further. Make a selection, select the layer mask thumbnail, and then go to **Select > Intersect with Selection**.
- **Using Blend If for Masking:** The **Blend If** sliders in the **Layer Style** dialog box allow you to create masks based on the luminosity of the current layer or the underlying layers. This can be useful for blending images or creating special effects.
- **Luminosity Masks:** Luminosity masks are selections based on the brightness values of an image. They are useful for making targeted adjustments to highlights, midtones, or shadows. You can create luminosity masks manually or using third-party actions or panels.
- **Apply Image:** This command allows you to blend the layer with other layers using various blending modes and an optional mask.

5.12 Using AI to Generate Complex Masks

Photoshop 2025 is expected to further integrate AI capabilities to assist with mask creation. Here are some potential ways AI could be used:

- **Automatic Mask Generation:** AI could analyze an image and automatically generate masks for different objects or regions, even those with complex edges. Imagine selecting "Generate Mask for Sky" or "Generate Mask for People" and having Photoshop do the hard work for you.
- **AI-Powered Refine Edge:** The Refine Edge Brush could be enhanced with AI to make it even more accurate and intelligent, especially when dealing with difficult areas like hair or fur.
- **Content-Aware Masking:** Similar to Content-Aware Fill, AI could be used to intelligently fill in or modify masks based on the surrounding image content.
- **Mask Suggestions:** Photoshop could suggest potential masks based on the image content and your editing actions.

This concludes Chapter 5! You've now gained a comprehensive understanding of selections and masking in Photoshop. You've explored various selection tools, learned how to refine selections with the Select and Mask workspace, discovered the power of layer masks and vector masks, and even touched on advanced masking techniques. You're well on your way to mastering one of the most essential aspects of Photoshop. In the next chapter, we'll dive into the world of image retouching and explore the tools and techniques for enhancing and repairing your photos.

Creating and Importing Documents

Now that you have a good grasp of the Photoshop workspace, selections, and masking, it's time to learn how to create new documents and import existing images. This chapter will cover the essential steps for setting up new documents with the correct size, resolution, and color mode, as well as how to open and import images from your computer, scanners, and cameras.

6.1 Creating a New Document: Setting Up Size, Resolution, and Color Mode

When you launch Photoshop, you can create a new document by clicking the "Create new" button on the welcome screen. If Photoshop is already running with no documents open, you can also access the welcome screen by going to File > New. Or, if a document is already open, go to **File > New** or use the keyboard shortcut **Ctrl+N (Windows)** or **Cmd+N (macOS)**. This will open the **New Document** dialog box.

The New Document Dialog Box:

This dialog box is where you define the initial properties of your new document. It has several sections:

- **Recent:** Shows recently used document sizes.
- **Saved:** Allows you to save frequently used document settings as presets.
- **Photo, Print, Art & Illustration, Web, Mobile, Film & Video:** These tabs provide preset document sizes for common use cases.

- **Document Preset Details:** This is where you fine-tune the settings for your new document:
    - **Preset Details:** Give your preset a descriptive name. This is especially helpful if you plan to save it for later use.
    - **Width and Height:** Specify the dimensions of your document. You can choose from various units, including pixels, inches, centimeters, millimeters, points, and picas.
    - **Orientation:** Choose between portrait (vertical) and landscape (horizontal) orientation.
    - **Artboards:** Check this option if you want to create a document with multiple artboards, which are like separate canvases within a single document. This is useful for designing for multiple screens or variations of a design.

- **Resolution:** Set the resolution of your document in pixels per inch (PPI). Remember:
    - **72 PPI:** Standard for web and screen images.
    - **300 PPI:** Standard for high-quality printing.

- **Color Mode:** Choose the appropriate color mode for your project:
    - **RGB:** For web and screen images.
    - **CMYK:** For print.
    - **Grayscale:** For black and white images.

- **Bitmap:** For line art (only black and white pixels).
- **Lab Color:** A device-independent color model.

o **Bit Depth:** Select the bit depth for your document (8-bit, 16-bit, or 32-bit). Higher bit depths offer more colors and greater editing flexibility but result in larger files.

o **Background Contents:** Choose the initial background color for your document:
- **White:** A solid white background.
- **Black:** A solid black background.
- **Background Color:** The currently selected background color in the Tools Panel.
- **Transparent:** No background color; the background will be transparent.
- **Custom:** Allows you to choose any color for the background.

o **Advanced Options:**
- **Color Profile:** Choose a color profile that defines the color space for your document. sRGB is common for web, Adobe RGB (1998) for print. If you're unsure, leave it at the default setting, which is usually your working color space defined in Photoshop's Color Settings.
- **Pixel Aspect Ratio:** Generally, leave this at "Square Pixels" unless you're working with specific video formats that require non-square pixels.

Creating the Document:

Once you've configured all the settings, click the **Create** button to create your new document.

6.2 Using Presets and Templates

Photoshop provides a variety of presets and templates to help you quickly create new documents with common settings.

Presets:
- **Predefined Settings:** Presets are predefined sets of document settings, such as size, resolution, and color mode.
- **Accessing Presets:** In the New Document dialog box, you'll find presets under the tabs (Photo, Print, Web, etc.).
- **Using Presets:** Click on a preset to automatically fill in the corresponding settings in the Document Preset Details section.
- **Saving Custom Presets:** After configuring your document settings, you can save them as a custom preset by clicking the **Save Preset** icon (a floppy disk with a plus sign) in the Preset Details section, giving it a name, and clicking Save Preset. Your custom preset will then appear in the **Saved** tab.

Templates:
- **Starting Points:** Templates are pre-designed documents that you can use as a starting point for your projects.

- **Adobe Stock Templates:** Photoshop provides access to a library of templates from Adobe Stock, including templates for brochures, flyers, business cards, social media graphics, and more.
- **Accessing Templates:**
  - In the New Document dialog box, click on the **Adobe Stock** tab.
  - You can search for templates by keyword or browse by category.
  - Click on a template to preview it.
  - If you want to use a template, click the **Download** button to download it from Adobe Stock (you may need to license it if it's a premium template).
  - Once downloaded, click the **Open** button to open the template in Photoshop.
- **Using Templates:** Templates often contain placeholder text, images, and layers that you can customize to fit your needs.

6.3 Opening Existing Images

There are several ways to open existing images in Photoshop:

- **File > Open:** Go to **File > Open** or use the keyboard shortcut **Ctrl+O (Windows)** or **Cmd+O (macOS)**. This will open a standard file browser dialog where you can navigate to the location of your image file and select it.
- **Double-Click in the Welcome Screen:** In the Welcome Screen, you can double-click on a recent file to open it.
- **Drag and Drop:** Drag an image file from your computer's file explorer (Finder on macOS) and drop it onto the Photoshop application window or icon.
- **Open As:** Go to **File > Open As** to open an image with a specific file format interpretation. This is useful if Photoshop is not automatically recognizing the correct format or if you want to open a file as a Smart Object.
- **Open Recent:** Go to **File > Open Recent** to access a list of recently opened files.
- **Supported File Formats:** Photoshop supports a wide range of image file formats, including JPEG, PNG, GIF, TIFF, PSD, PDF, and many more.

6.4 Importing Images from Scanners and Cameras

Photoshop can directly import images from scanners and cameras that are connected to your computer.

Importing from a Scanner:

1. **Install Scanner Drivers:** Make sure you have the latest drivers installed for your scanner.
2. **Connect the Scanner:** Connect your scanner to your computer and turn it on.
3. **Go to File > Import > WIA Support (Windows) or use Image Capture (macOS):**
   - **WIA (Windows Image Acquisition):** A standard interface for acquiring images from scanners and cameras on Windows.

- **Image Capture:** A built-in macOS application for importing images from scanners and cameras.
4. **Choose Your Scanner:** Select your scanner from the list of available devices.
5. **Preview and Scan:** You'll typically see a preview window where you can adjust scan settings such as resolution, color mode, and file format. Make any necessary adjustments and then click the **Scan** button.
6. **Import into Photoshop:** Once the scan is complete, the image should automatically open in Photoshop.

Importing from a Camera:

1. **Connect the Camera:** Connect your camera to your computer using a USB cable or insert the camera's memory card into a card reader.
2. **Turn on the Camera:** Make sure your camera is turned on and set to the appropriate mode for transferring images (often called "Playback" or "Transfer" mode).
3. **Use File > Get Photos from Camera (or similar, if available) or AutoPlay (Windows) / Image Capture (macOS):**
   - Some versions of Photoshop may have a direct import option under the File menu.
   - **AutoPlay (Windows):** If AutoPlay is enabled, a dialog box will pop up asking what you want to do with the connected device. You can choose to import photos using the default photo management application or directly into Photoshop (if the option is available).
   - **Image Capture (macOS):** Similar to scanning, Image Capture can also be used to import photos from cameras.
4. **Select Images to Import:** Choose the images you want to import from the camera or memory card.
5. **Choose Import Options:** You may be able to specify a destination folder, file naming conventions, and other import options.
6. **Import:** Click the **Import** or **Download** button to transfer the images to your computer. They should then open in Photoshop.
   Note: The exact steps for importing from scanners and cameras may vary slightly depending on your operating system, scanner/camera model, and the version of Photoshop you're using. Refer to your scanner/camera documentation or the Photoshop Help files for more specific instructions.

6.5 Placing Images as Smart Objects

In Chapter 4, you were introduced to Smart Objects, which are special layers that preserve an image's original data and allow for non-destructive editing. Placing images as Smart Objects is a good practice, especially when you're working with files from external sources or when you anticipate needing to resize or transform the image multiple times.

Methods for Placing Images as Smart Objects:
- **File > Place Embedded:**

1. Go to **File > Place Embedded...**
2. Navigate to the image file you want to place.
3. Select the file and click **Place**.
4. The image will be placed as a Smart Object in your current document. It's embedded within the Photoshop file, meaning a copy of the image data is stored within the PSD.

- **File > Place Linked:**
  1. Go to **File > Place Linked...**
  2. Navigate to the image file you want to place.
  3. Select the file and click **Place**.
  4. The image will be placed as a Smart Object that's linked to the original external file. This means that if you update the original file, the Smart Object in Photoshop will automatically update as well. This can be useful for maintaining consistency across multiple projects or when working with elements that might be revised externally.

- **Drag and Drop (from File Explorer/Finder):**
  1. You can drag an image file from your computer's file explorer (Finder on macOS) and drop it directly onto your Photoshop canvas.
  2. By default, dragging and dropping usually creates a Smart Object (either embedded or linked, depending on your Photoshop settings and the file type).

Benefits of Placing as Smart Objects:
- **Non-Destructive Transformations:** Scale, rotate, skew, and distort the image without losing quality.
- **Non-Destructive Filters (Smart Filters):** Apply filters that remain editable.
- **Linked Smart Objects:** Update the Smart Object by editing the original external file.

6.6 Working with Artboards for Multi-Screen Design

Artboards are a powerful feature in Photoshop that's particularly useful for designing user interfaces (UIs), websites, and mobile apps, or any project that requires multiple variations of a design within a single document.

What are Artboards?
- Think of artboards as separate canvases within a single Photoshop document.
- Each artboard can have its own dimensions, resolution, and even color mode.
- You can design for different screen sizes or create variations of a design side-by-side.

Creating Artboards:

- **During Document Creation:** When creating a new document (**File > New**), check the **Artboards** option in the New Document dialog box.
- **Converting an Existing Document:** You can convert a regular document into an artboard-based document. Select the **Artboard Tool** from the Tools Panel. Then, in the Options Bar, select Document from the Convert To: dropdown menu and click Convert.

- **Using the Artboard Tool (V):**
  - Select the Artboard Tool from the Tools Panel (it's nested with the Move Tool).
  - Click and drag in the document window to create a new artboard.
  - In the Options bar, you can choose from preset artboard sizes (e.g., iPhone, iPad, web sizes) or define custom dimensions.
- **From Layers:** Select one or more layers in the Layers Panel and then go to Layer > New > Artboard from Layers.

Managing Artboards:

- **Selecting Artboards:**
  - Click on the artboard's name in the Layers Panel.
  - Click on the artboard's name label in the document window.
  - Use the Artboard Tool to click and select an artboard.

- **Resizing Artboards:**
  - Select the Artboard Tool, click on an artboard, and then drag the handles to resize it.
  - Enter specific dimensions in the Options Bar.

- **Duplicating Artboards:**
  - **Alt-drag (Windows) / Option-drag (macOS)** the artboard's name in the Layers Panel or in the document window.
  - Select the Artboard Tool, then select the artboard you would like to duplicate. In the Options Bar, select a position for your new artboard relative to the currently selected one and click the plus button.

- **Deleting Artboards:** Select the artboard and press **Delete**, or right-click the artboard's name and choose **Delete Artboard**.
- **Arranging Artboards:** Drag artboards in the document window to reposition them.
- **Aligning and Distributing Artboards:** Use the alignment and distribution options in the Options Bar when the Artboard Tool is active.

Layers Panel with Artboards:

- The Layers Panel displays artboards as top-level groups.
- Layers and groups within an artboard are nested under that artboard's group.
- You can drag layers between artboards.

Exporting Artboards:

- **File > Export > Artboards to Files:** Exports each artboard as a separate file.
- **File > Export > Artboards to PDF:** Exports all artboards into a single PDF document.
- **File > Export > Export As:** Allows more granular control over export settings for each artboard.
- **Right-click** on an artboard's name in the Layers Panel and choose **Export As** or **Quick Export as [format]**.

6.7 Saving Your Work: File Formats and Options

Saving your work regularly is crucial. Photoshop offers a variety of file formats, each with its own strengths and weaknesses.

Saving for the First Time:
- **File > Save As:** This opens the Save As dialog box, where you can choose the file format, location, and name for your document.
- **Saving Subsequent Changes:**
- **File > Save:** Or use the shortcut **Ctrl+S (Windows) / Cmd+S (macOS)**. This will overwrite the previously saved version of your file.

Common File Formats:
- **PSD (Photoshop Document):**
  - Photoshop's native format.
  - Preserves all layers, adjustments, masks, and other editing information.
  - Use this format for ongoing projects that you'll continue to edit in Photoshop.

- **PSB (Photoshop Big Document):**
  - Similar to PSD but supports much larger files (up to 300,000 x 300,000 pixels).
  - Use this when your document exceeds the size limitations of PSD.

- **JPEG (JPG):**
  - A compressed format commonly used for web images and digital photos.
  - Offers a good balance between image quality and file size.
  - Does not support transparency or layers.

- **PNG:**
  - A lossless format that supports transparency.
  - Ideal for web graphics, logos, and images with sharp lines and text.

- **GIF:**
  - Supports transparency and animation but is limited to 256 colors.
  - Suitable for simple web graphics and small animations.

- **TIFF (TIF):**

- A high-quality format often used for print and archiving.
- Supports layers, transparency, and various compression options.

- **PDF (Portable Document Format):**
    - A versatile format that can preserve layers, vector graphics, and text.
    - Suitable for sharing documents that need to be viewed or printed consistently across different platforms.

Save As Dialog Box Options:
- **File Name:** Enter a descriptive name for your file.
- **Format:** Choose the desired file format from the drop-down menu.
- **Save Options:** Depending on the chosen format, you may have additional options:
    - **Embed Color Profile:** Embeds the color profile in the image, ensuring consistent color reproduction.
    - **Layers:** (For formats that support layers) Preserves the layers in the saved file.
    - **As a Copy:** Saves a copy of the document without changing the currently open file.
    - **Alpha Channels:** Preserves any alpha channels (selections saved as channels) in your document.
    - **Spot Colors:** Preserves spot colors.

- **Image Options (JPEG):**
    - **Quality:** Controls the level of compression. Higher quality means less compression and a larger file size.
    - **Format Options:** Baseline ("Standard") is the most common. Baseline Optimized provides slightly better compression. Progressive allows the image to be displayed gradually as it downloads, which can be useful for web images.

- **PNG Options:**
    - **Interlace:** Similar to Progressive for JPEG, this allows the PNG to display gradually.

- **TIFF Options:**
    - **Image Compression:** None (no compression), LZW (lossless), ZIP (lossless), JPEG (lossy).
    - **Pixel Order:** Interleaved is the most common.
    - **Byte Order:** Choose the appropriate byte order for your operating system.
    - **Save Image Pyramid:** Creates multiple versions of the image at different resolutions, which can speed up loading in some applications.
    - **Layer Compression:** RLE is a fast and simple lossless compression. ZIP provides better compression but may be slower.

6.8 Importing and Using AI-Generated Assets

Photoshop 2025 and the broader Creative Cloud ecosystem are increasingly integrating AI-powered features. This includes the ability to import and use assets generated by AI tools, potentially from Adobe Firefly or other generative AI platforms.

Potential Sources of AI-Generated Assets:
- **Adobe Firefly (or similar):** Adobe's generative AI platform might offer the ability to generate images, textures, patterns, or even 3D objects that can be directly imported into Photoshop.
- **Third-Party AI Tools:** You might use other AI image generators and then import the results into Photoshop.

Importing AI-Generated Assets:
The specific methods for importing AI-generated assets might vary depending on the source and the type of asset. Here are some possibilities:
- **Direct Integration:** There might be a direct integration between Photoshop and a generative AI platform, allowing you to browse, select, and import assets without leaving Photoshop. This could be through a dedicated panel or a menu command.
- **Creative Cloud Libraries:** AI-generated assets might be saved to your Creative Cloud Libraries, making them accessible across all your Creative Cloud applications, including Photoshop.
- **File > Place:** You might be able to import AI-generated images using the **File > Place Embedded** or **File > Place Linked** commands, just like any other image file.
- **Drag and Drop:** Dragging and dropping an AI-generated asset from a web browser or file explorer into Photoshop might be supported.
- **Clipboard:** Copying an image from an AI generation tool and pasting it into Photoshop (Edit > Paste).

Using AI-Generated Assets in Photoshop:
Once imported, you can work with AI-generated assets just like any other image or Smart Object:
- **Transformations:** Scale, rotate, and distort the asset.
- **Adjustments:** Apply color and tonal adjustments.
- **Filters:** Use filters to enhance or stylize the asset.
- **Masking:** Create masks to selectively hide or reveal parts of the asset.
- **Compositing:** Combine the asset with other images and elements to create a composite.

Considerations:
- **Resolution and Quality:** The resolution and quality of AI-generated assets will vary depending on the source and the generation parameters.

- **Licensing:** Be aware of the licensing terms for any AI-generated assets you use, especially if you're using them for commercial purposes.
- **Ethical Implications:** Consider the ethical implications of using AI-generated content, particularly in relation to copyright, originality, and the potential impact on human artists.

This completes Chapter 6! You now have a solid understanding of how to create and manage documents in Photoshop, from setting up new files to importing images and working with artboards. You've also learned about the various file formats and saving options, as well as the emerging possibilities of using AI-generated assets. In the next chapter, we'll explore the essential retouching tools, putting your knowledge into practice to enhance and repair your images.

You've Reached the Middle... But Your Photoshop Journey Has Just Begun!

Congratulations on completing **"ADOBE PHOTOSHOP 2025 USER GUIDE: THE COMPREHENSIVE BEGINNER TO EXPERT ILLUSTRATIVE MANUAL TO MASTERING ADOBE PHOTOSHOP 2025 WITH UPDATED SHORTCUTS, TIPS & TRICKS"**! We sincerely hope this book has been a valuable resource on your journey to mastering Adobe Photoshop 2025. From understanding the fundamentals of the interface to exploring advanced techniques like non-destructive editing, retouching, color adjustments, filters, 3D, and even the exciting possibilities of AI, you've gained a comprehensive skillset that will empower you to bring your creative visions to life.

But learning Photoshop is an ongoing adventure, a continuous process of exploration, experimentation, and growth. This book has provided you with a strong foundation, but the true magic happens when you apply these skills, develop your own unique style, and continue to push the boundaries of your creativity.

We'd Love to Hear from You!

Your feedback is incredibly important to us. If this book has helped you on your Photoshop journey, we'd be extremely grateful if you could take a few minutes to **leave an honest review on Amazon**. Your review will not only help other aspiring Photoshop users discover this guide but also provide us with valuable insights to improve future editions.

Why Your Review Matters:

- **Helps Others:** Your experience can help others decide if this book is right for them. Whether you're a complete beginner or a seasoned user, your perspective is valuable.
- **Supports the Author:** Reviews help boost the book's visibility on Amazon, allowing it to reach a wider audience.
- **Improves Future Editions:** Your feedback, both positive and constructive, helps us understand what worked well and what could be improved in future updates.

What to Include in Your Review:

- **Your Background:** Briefly mention your skill level with Photoshop (beginner, intermediate, advanced).
- **What You Learned:** Share specific examples of what you found most helpful or what new skills you gained.
- **How the Book Helped You:** Describe how this book has impacted your Photoshop workflow or creative projects.
- **Any Suggestions:** If you have any suggestions for improvement, we're all ears!

Leaving a review is easy:

1. Go to the book's page on Amazon.

2. Scroll down to the "Customer Reviews" section.
3. Click on "Write a customer review."
4. Rate the book and share your thoughts in the review box.
5. Click "Submit".

Thank you for taking the time to share your experience. We truly appreciate your support!

Now go forth and create! We can't wait to see what amazing things you'll achieve with your newfound Photoshop skills. Remember to keep practicing, keep exploring, and never stop learning. The world of digital art and design is full of endless possibilities, and you now have the tools to make your mark.

Happy Photoshopping!

Working with Smart Objects

Smart Objects are one of the most powerful and versatile features in Photoshop. They provide a non-destructive way to work with images, filters, and transformations, preserving the original data and allowing for maximum flexibility. This chapter will explore what Smart Objects are, why you should use them, and how to create, edit, and replace their contents.

7.1 What are Smart Objects and Why Use Them?

Smart Objects are special layers that contain image data from raster or vector images. They act like containers, encapsulating the original image data within the Photoshop document. Think of a Smart Object as a separate, embedded Photoshop document within your main document.

Why Use Smart Objects?
- **Non-Destructive Transformations:** You can scale, rotate, skew, distort, or apply perspective transformations to a Smart Object *without* permanently altering the original image data. You can always revert to the original or adjust the transformations later.
- **Non-Destructive Filters (Smart Filters):** When you apply a filter to a Smart Object, it becomes a *Smart Filter*. Smart Filters are editable; you can change their settings, reorder them, mask them, or remove them entirely without affecting the original image.

- **Linked Smart Objects:** You can create Linked Smart Objects that are connected to an external file. When you update the external file, all instances of the Linked Smart Object in your Photoshop document are automatically updated. This is incredibly useful for:
  - **Consistency:** Maintaining consistency across multiple designs or layouts.
  - **Efficiency:** Updating a single source file instead of multiple instances.
  - **Collaboration:** Allowing multiple people to work on different parts of a project while ensuring that shared elements remain synchronized.
- **Embedded Smart Objects:** These are self-contained and not linked to an external file. They are useful when you want to include an image within your Photoshop document and maintain its editability without relying on an external file.
- **Place Vector Artwork:** You can place vector artwork (e.g., from Adobe Illustrator) as Smart Objects, preserving their vector editability within Photoshop.
- **Improved File Organization:** Smart Objects can help keep your Layers Panel organized, especially when working with complex composites.

7.2 Creating Smart Objects

There are several ways to create Smart Objects in Photoshop:

- **Converting Existing Layers:**
  1. Select the layer or layers you want to convert in the Layers Panel.
  2. Right-click (Windows) or Control-click (macOS) on the selected layer(s).
  3. Choose **Convert to Smart Object**.

- **Placing Files as Smart Objects:**
  1. Go to **File > Place Embedded** or **File > Place Linked**.

  2. Select the image file you want to place.

  3. Click **Place**.
     - **Place Embedded:** Embeds a copy of the image data within your Photoshop document.
     - **Place Linked:** Creates a link to the external image file.

- **Opening Images as Smart Objects:**
  - Go to **File > Open As Smart Object**.
  - Select the image file.
  - Click **Open**.

Identifying Smart Objects:

Smart Object layers have a small icon in the lower-right corner of their layer thumbnail in the Layers Panel. This icon helps you distinguish them from regular pixel layers.

7.3 Editing the Contents of a Smart Object

Since a Smart Object acts as a container, you need to open it separately to edit its contents directly.

How to Edit the Contents:
- **Double-click the Smart Object's thumbnail** in the Layers Panel.
- **Right-click (Windows) or Control-click (macOS)** on the Smart Object layer and choose **Edit Contents**.

What Happens:
- The Smart Object will open in a new document window. This is a temporary PSB file (Photoshop Big Document format) for embedded Smart Objects, or the original file for linked Smart Objects.
- You can make any edits you like to the contents of the Smart Object in this separate window. You can add layers, paint, apply adjustments, etc.
- When you're finished, go to **File > Save** (or **Ctrl+S / Cmd+S**). This saves the changes to the embedded Smart Object or updates the linked file.
- Close the Smart Object document window.

Updating the Main Document:
- The changes you made to the Smart Object's contents will be reflected in your main Photoshop document.
- Any transformations or Smart Filters applied to the Smart Object will be automatically updated to reflect the changes.

7.4 Replacing the Contents of a Smart Object

One of the great advantages of Smart Objects is the ability to easily replace their contents while preserving any applied transformations or filters.

How to Replace Contents:
- **Right-click (Windows) or Control-click (macOS)** on the Smart Object layer in the Layers Panel.
- Choose **Replace Contents**.
- Select the new image file you want to use.
- Click **Place**.

What Happens:

- The original contents of the Smart Object are replaced with the new image.
- The new image will inherit any transformations, Smart Filters, or layer styles that were applied to the original Smart Object.

Use Cases for Replacing Contents:
- **Swapping out images in a template:** This is useful for creating variations of a design quickly.
- **Updating a linked Smart Object:** If you've made changes to the external file linked to a Smart Object, you can use "Relink to File" to update it.
- **Experimenting with different images:** You can quickly try out different images in the same layout without having to reapply transformations or filters.

Example:
Imagine you have a Smart Object of a product photo in your design. You've scaled and rotated the Smart Object and applied a drop shadow layer style. If you want to use a different product photo, you can simply replace the contents of the Smart Object. The new photo will automatically be scaled, rotated, and have the drop shadow applied, matching the original Smart Object's settings.

7.5 Converting Smart Objects Back to Layers

While Smart Objects offer many advantages, there are times when you might need to convert them back to regular pixel layers. This process is called **rasterizing**.

When to Rasterize a Smart Object:
- **Pixel-Level Editing:** If you need to directly edit the pixels of a Smart Object using tools like the Brush, Eraser, or Clone Stamp (you can perform these edits *within* the Smart Object, but not directly on the Smart Object layer itself).

- **Reducing File Size:** In some cases, rasterizing a Smart Object might reduce the overall file size, especially if the Smart Object contains a large, embedded image and you've made significant transformations to it.
- **Compatibility:** Some older versions of Photoshop or other applications might not fully support Smart Objects.

How to Rasterize a Smart Object:

- **Right-click (Windows) or Control-click (macOS)** on the Smart Object layer in the Layers Panel.
- Choose **Rasterize Layer**.

Important Considerations:

- **Loss of Non-Destructive Editing:** Once you rasterize a Smart Object, you lose the ability to edit the original image data, transformations, and Smart Filters non-destructively.
- **Rasterizing Smart Filters:** If the Smart Object has Smart Filters applied, you'll be prompted to rasterize the filters as well. This means the filter settings will be permanently applied to the pixels and will no longer be editable.

Alternatives to Rasterizing (When Possible):

- **Edit the Contents:** Instead of rasterizing, double-click the Smart Object thumbnail to edit its contents directly. This preserves the non-destructive nature of the Smart Object.
- **Duplicate and Rasterize:** If you need a rasterized version of the Smart Object but also want to keep the original, duplicate the Smart Object layer (**Ctrl+J / Cmd+J**) and then rasterize the copy.

7.6 Benefits of Smart Objects for Non-Destructive Editing

The core strength of Smart Objects lies in their ability to facilitate a non-destructive workflow. Let's recap the key benefits in this context:

- **Preserving Original Image Data:** The original image data within a Smart Object is protected, regardless of how many transformations or filters you apply.
- **Editable Transformations:** You can freely scale, rotate, skew, distort, or change the perspective of a Smart Object without degrading the image quality. You can always revert to the original or fine-tune the transformations later.
- **Editable Filters (Smart Filters):** Filters applied to Smart Objects remain fully editable. You can change the filter settings, reorder them, adjust their opacity, or even mask them without permanently altering the underlying image.
- **Flexibility and Experimentation:** Smart Objects encourage experimentation because you can try out different looks and effects without worrying about making irreversible changes.
- **Maintaining Image Quality:** By avoiding repeated rasterization and reapplication of transformations and filters, you preserve the best possible image quality throughout your editing process.

Smart Objects become even more powerful when combined with filters and adjustment layers.

Smart Filters:

- **Applying Smart Filters:**

1. Select a Smart Object layer in the Layers Panel.

2. Go to **Filter** in the Menu Bar and choose a filter.
    - The filter will be applied as a Smart Filter, appearing as a separate, editable item beneath the Smart Object layer in the Layers Panel.

- **Editing Smart Filters:**
    1. **Double-click** the name of the Smart Filter in the Layers Panel to reopen its settings dialog and make adjustments.
    2. **Change the Blending Mode or Opacity:** Click the small icon with two sliders next to the filter's name in the Layers Panel to adjust its blending mode or opacity.
    3. **Hide or Show:** Click the eye icon next to the Smart Filter to temporarily hide or show its effect.
    4. **Reorder:** Drag and drop Smart Filters in the Layers Panel to change their order of application.
    5. **Delete:** Drag the Smart Filter to the trash can icon at the bottom of the Layers Panel or select it and press **Delete**.

- **Masking Smart Filters:**
    1. Each Smart Filter has a mask associated with it (the white thumbnail next to the filter's name).
    2. You can paint on the mask with black to hide the filter's effect in specific areas, white to reveal it, or shades of gray to partially apply the effect.

Adjustment Layers with Smart Objects:

While you typically apply adjustment layers *above* the layers you want to affect, you can also clip adjustment layers to Smart Objects.

- **Clipping Adjustment Layers:**

1. Create an adjustment layer above the Smart Object layer.
2. **Alt-click (Windows) / Option-click (macOS)** on the line between the adjustment layer and the Smart Object layer in the Layers Panel.
   - This will clip the adjustment layer to the Smart Object, meaning the adjustment will only affect the contents of the Smart Object.

Example Workflow: Non-Destructive Photo Editing with Smart Objects

Here's an example of how you might use Smart Objects, Smart Filters, and adjustment layers for a non-destructive photo editing workflow:

1. **Convert to Smart Object:** Open your image in Photoshop and convert the Background layer to a Smart Object.
2. **Apply Smart Filters:**
   - Apply a **Camera Raw Filter (Filter > Camera Raw Filter)** to make initial adjustments to exposure, contrast, highlights, shadows, etc.
   - Apply a **Gaussian Blur** filter (**Filter > Blur > Gaussian Blur**) to soften the image slightly.
   - Apply an **Unsharp Mask** filter (**Filter > Sharpen > Unsharp Mask**) to add a touch of sharpening.
3. **Add Adjustment Layers:**
   - Add a **Curves** adjustment layer clipped to the Smart Object to fine-tune the tonal contrast.
   - Add a **Hue/Saturation** adjustment layer clipped to the Smart Object to adjust the colors.
4. **Mask Smart Filters:** If needed, paint on the Smart Filter masks to selectively apply the filters. For example, you might mask the Gaussian Blur filter to only blur the background of the image.

Benefits of this Workflow:

- You can go back and readjust any of the Camera Raw settings at any time.
- You can change the blur amount or sharpening settings without degrading the image.
- You can fine-tune the Curves and Hue/Saturation adjustments without permanently altering the pixel data.
- You can easily hide, show, or delete any of the Smart Filters or adjustment layers.

This concludes Chapter 7. You've now gained a deep understanding of Smart Objects and their role in non-destructive editing. You've learned how to create and edit Smart Objects, replace their contents, convert them back to regular layers, and leverage their power in conjunction with Smart

Filters and adjustment layers. In the next chapter, we'll explore a variety of retouching tools, enabling you to enhance and repair your images with precision.

Essential Retouching Tools

Retouching is a crucial part of many image editing workflows. Whether you're removing blemishes from a portrait, repairing damage in an old photograph, or eliminating unwanted objects from a scene, Photoshop offers a powerful set of tools to help you achieve seamless results. This chapter will cover some of the most essential retouching tools: the Healing Brush, Spot Healing Brush, Patch Tool, Clone Stamp Tool, and Content-Aware Move Tool.

8.1 The Healing Brush: Removing Blemishes and Imperfections

The Healing Brush Tool is a versatile tool for removing blemishes, dust spots, scratches, and other imperfections from your images. It works by blending the texture and color of a sampled area with the area you're retouching.

How to Use the Healing Brush:

1. **Select the Healing Brush Tool (J)** from the Tools Panel. It's grouped with the Spot Healing Brush, Patch Tool, and others.
2. **Adjust the Brush Settings in the Options Bar:**
   * **Brush Size:** Adjust the size of the brush tip using the **[** and **]** keys or the **Size** slider in the Options Bar.
   * **Hardness:** Controls the softness of the brush edge. A lower hardness value creates a softer, more gradual transition.
   * **Spacing:** Determines the distance between brush strokes.
   * **Mode:** Usually set to **Normal**. Other modes like Replace can be useful in special cases.
   * **Source:** Choose between **Sampled** (you manually select the source area) or **Pattern** (uses a predefined pattern). For most retouching, you'll use **Sampled**.
   * **Sample:** Current Layer will only sample from the active layer. Current & Below will sample from the active layer and any visible layers below it. All Layers will sample from all visible layers regardless of which is selected.
   * **Aligned:** When checked, the sampling point moves relative to the brush cursor as you paint. When unchecked, the sampling point returns to the original location each time you release the mouse button.
   * **Diffusion:** This slider controls how quickly the pasted pixels are adapted to their surroundings.

3. **Sample a Source Area:** Hold down **Alt (Windows) / Option (macOS)** and click on an area of the image that has a texture and color similar to the area you want to retouch. This is your source area.

4. **Paint Over the Imperfection:** Release the **Alt/Option** key and paint over the blemish or imperfection you want to remove.

How it Works:

The Healing Brush intelligently blends the texture from the source area with the color and luminosity of the area you're painting over, creating a more seamless repair than simply copying pixels.

Tips for Using the Healing Brush:

- **Choose a source area that closely matches the area you're retouching** in terms of texture, color, and lighting.
- **Use a brush size that's slightly larger than the imperfection** you're trying to remove.
- **Work in small strokes** rather than trying to fix everything at once.
- **Resample frequently** as you move to different areas of the image.
- **Adjust the Hardness** to control the blending. A softer brush often produces more natural results.

8.2 The Spot Healing Brush: Quick Fixes with AI

The Spot Healing Brush Tool is similar to the Healing Brush, but it's even easier to use because it automatically samples the source area for you. It leverages AI (similar to Content-Aware Fill) to analyze the surrounding pixels and create a seamless repair.

How to Use the Spot Healing Brush:
1. **Select the Spot Healing Brush Tool (J)** from the Tools Panel.
2. **Adjust the Brush Settings in the Options Bar:**
   - **Brush Size:** Adjust the size of the brush tip.
   - **Hardness:** Controls the softness of the brush edge.
   - **Spacing:** Determines the distance between brush strokes.

   o **Type:**
   3. **Proximity Match:** Samples pixels around the edge of the brush stroke.
   4. **Create Texture:** Generates a texture based on the surrounding area.
   5. **Content-Aware:** Uses AI to analyze the surrounding area and create a more intelligent fill. This is generally the most effective option.

   o **Sample All Layers:** When checked, the tool considers pixels from all visible layers when making the repair. When unchecked, it only samples from the currently active layer.

6. **Click or paint over the imperfection.** Photoshop will automatically analyze the surrounding area and attempt to seamlessly fill in the area.

Tips for Using the Spot Healing Brush:
1. **Use a brush size that's slightly larger than the blemish.**
2. **Content-Aware usually provides the best results.**
3. **For larger areas, you may need to click or paint multiple times.**
4. **The Spot Healing Brush works best on small, isolated imperfections.** For larger or more complex areas, the Healing Brush or Patch Tool might be more suitable.

8.3 The Patch Tool: Seamlessly Replacing Areas

The Patch Tool allows you to select an area you want to repair and then drag that selection to a source area to sample from. It then blends the texture, color, and luminosity of the source area with the original area, creating a seamless patch.

How to Use the Patch Tool:
1. **Select the Patch Tool (J)** from the Tools Panel.
2. **Choose the Patch Mode in the Options Bar:**
   - **Normal:** Replaces the destination with a blend of the source and the original content.

- **Content-Aware:** Uses AI to create a more intelligent and seamless blend.

3. **Choose Source or Destination:**
   - **Source:** You draw a selection around the area you want to *repair* (the destination) and then drag the selection to the area you want to sample *from* (the source).
   - **Destination:** You draw a selection around the area you want to *sample from* (the source) and then drag that selection to the area you want to *repair* (the destination). This option can be used to duplicate image content.

4. **Draw a selection** around the area you want to repair or sample from.
5. **Drag the selection** to the source area. As you drag, you'll see a preview of the patched area.
6. **Release the mouse button** to apply the patch.

Options Bar Settings:
- **New Selection, Add to Selection, Subtract from Selection, Intersect with Selection:** Similar to other selection tools.
- **Patch:** Normal or Content-Aware.
- **Source/Destination:** Choose which area is the source and which is the destination.
- **Transparent:** When using the Destination mode, checking this option will prevent the tool from copying any transparent pixels from the source to the destination.
- **Diffusion:** This slider controls how quickly the pasted pixels are adapted to their surroundings.

Tips for Using the Patch Tool:
- **Content-Aware mode often produces better results**, especially for complex areas.
- **Use a feathered selection** to create a softer transition between the patched area and the surrounding image.
- **Make sure the source area is large enough** to provide sufficient texture and detail for the patch.
- **The Patch Tool works well for repairing larger areas** than the Healing Brush or Spot Healing Brush.

8.4 The Clone Stamp Tool: Duplicating Image Areas

The Clone Stamp Tool allows you to copy pixels from one area of an image to another. It's useful for removing unwanted objects, duplicating elements, or filling in missing areas.

How to Use the Clone Stamp Tool:
1. **Select the Clone Stamp Tool (S)** from the Tools Panel.
2. **Adjust the Brush Settings in the Options Bar:**

- **Brush Size, Hardness, Spacing:** Similar to the Healing Brush.
- **Mode:** Usually set to **Normal**.
- **Opacity:** Controls the transparency of the cloned pixels.
- **Flow:** Controls the rate at which the cloned pixels are applied.
- **Aligned:** When checked, the sampling point moves relative to the brush cursor as you paint. When unchecked, the sampling point returns to the original location each time you release the mouse button.
- **Sample:** Choose which layers to sample from: Current Layer, Current & Below, or All Layers.

3. **Sample a Source Area:** Hold down **Alt (Windows) / Option (macOS)** and click on the area you want to clone from.
4. **Paint over the area** where you want to apply the cloned pixels.

Clone Source Panel:

The Clone Source Panel (**Window > Clone Source**) provides advanced options for the Clone Stamp Tool:
- **Multiple Clone Sources:** You can define up to five different clone sources and switch between them.
- **Source Overlays:** You can display an overlay of the source area as you paint, making it easier to align the cloned pixels.
- **Transformations:** You can scale, rotate, and flip the clone source before applying it.

Tips for Using the Clone Stamp Tool:

- **Choose a source area that closely matches the area you're painting over** in terms of color, texture, and lighting.
- **Use a soft brush** to create a more gradual transition between the cloned pixels and the surrounding area.
- **Resample frequently**, especially when cloning complex patterns or textures.
- **Use the Clone Source Panel** for more control over the cloning process.

8.5 The Content-Aware Move Tool: Repositioning Elements Intelligently

The Content-Aware Move Tool allows you to select and move an object within an image, and Photoshop will automatically fill in the background behind the moved object using Content-Aware technology.

How to Use the Content-Aware Move Tool:

1. **Select the Content-Aware Move Tool (J)** from the Tools Panel (it's grouped with the Healing Brush tools).
2. **Choose the Mode in the Options Bar:**
   - **Move:** Moves the selected object and fills the original location with Content-Aware Fill.
   - **Extend:** Extends or expands the selected object.

3. **Draw a selection** around the object you want to move or extend.
4. **Drag the selection** to the new location.
5. **Release the mouse button.** Photoshop will analyze the surrounding area and attempt to seamlessly fill in the background.
6. Adjust the **Structure** and **Color** options in the Options Bar to fine-tune the adaptation of the moved object to its new surroundings.
7. Press **Enter** or click the checkmark in the Options Bar to commit the change.

Options Bar Settings:

- **Mode:** Move or Extend.
- **Sample All Layers:** When checked, the tool considers pixels from all visible layers.
- **Transform on Drop:** When checked, you will see a bounding box around the moved object after releasing the mouse button. You can use the bounding box to further transform (scale, rotate, etc.) the moved object before committing the change.
- **Adaptation:** This controls how strictly the moved object will adhere to surrounding patterns.
  - **Very Strict:** The moved object will adhere closely to existing patterns.
  - **Very Loose:** The moved object will blend more loosely with the surrounding area.

Tips for Using the Content-Aware Move Tool:

- **Make a loose selection** around the object you want to move. It doesn't have to be precise.
- **Content-Aware Move works best when the background is relatively uniform.**
- **You may need to do some additional cleanup** with the Healing Brush or Clone Stamp Tool after using the Content-Aware Move Tool, especially if the background is complex.

8.6 The Red Eye Tool: Correcting Red Eye in Photos

The Red Eye Tool is a specialized tool for quickly fixing the red-eye effect that often occurs in flash photography when the flash reflects off the subject's retinas.

How to Use the Red Eye Tool:

1. **Select the Red Eye Tool (J)** from the Tools Panel. It's grouped with the other healing tools.
2. **Adjust the settings in the Options Bar:**
   - **Pupil Size:** Controls the size of the area affected by the tool.
   - **Darken Amount:** Determines how much the red areas will be darkened.

3. **Click on the red areas of the eyes in your photo.** Photoshop will automatically detect and correct the red-eye.

Tips for Using the Red Eye Tool:

- **Zoom in** on the eyes for more precise correction.
- **Start with the default settings** and adjust the Pupil Size and Darken Amount if needed.
- **In some cases, you may need to click multiple times** to completely remove the red-eye.
- The Red Eye Tool can also be used on animals, though the results may vary depending on the color of the animal's eyes.

8.7 Blur, Sharpen, and Smudge Tools: Fine-Tuning Details

These tools allow you to selectively blur, sharpen, or smudge areas of your image.

- **Blur Tool:** Softens edges or reduces detail by decreasing the contrast between adjacent pixels.
  - **Use Cases:** Softening skin, creating a shallow depth-of-field effect, reducing noise.
- **Sharpen Tool:** Increases the contrast between adjacent pixels, making edges appear more defined.
  - **Use Cases:** Enhancing details, making an image appear sharper (use with caution, as over-sharpening can introduce artifacts).
- **Smudge Tool:** Mixes and blends pixels together, as if you were smudging wet paint.
  - **Use Cases:** Smoothing out areas, creating artistic effects, blending colors.

How to Use the Blur, Sharpen, and Smudge Tools:

1. **Select the desired tool** from the Tools Panel.
2. **Adjust the brush settings in the Options Bar:**
   - **Brush Size, Hardness:** Similar to other brush-based tools.
   - **Mode:** (For Blur and Sharpen) Normally set to **Normal**.
   - **Strength:** Controls the intensity of the effect. A lower strength produces a more subtle effect.

- **Sample All Layers:** When checked, the tools will consider pixels from all visible layers.
- **Finger Painting:** (Smudge Tool Only) When checked, the Smudge tool starts by smudging with the foreground color.
- **Protect Detail:** (Sharpen Tool Only) When checked, this option attempts to minimize pixelation when sharpening.

3. **Paint over the areas** you want to blur, sharpen, or smudge.

Tips:
- **Use a low Strength setting** and build up the effect gradually.
- **Zoom in** to work on details.
- **Use a soft brush** for a more natural-looking result.
- **Be careful not to overdo it**, especially with the Sharpen tool, as it can easily introduce unwanted artifacts.

8.8 Dodge and Burn Tools: Lightening and Darkening Areas

The Dodge and Burn tools are used to selectively lighten (dodge) or darken (burn) areas of an image, mimicking traditional darkroom techniques. They are often used for enhancing highlights and shadows, sculpting features, and adding depth to an image.

- **Dodge Tool (O):** Lightens areas of the image.
- **Burn Tool (O):** Darkens areas of the image.

How to Use the Dodge and Burn Tools:
1. **Select the Dodge or Burn Tool (O)** from the Tools Panel.
2. **Adjust the brush settings in the Options Bar:**
   - **Brush Size, Hardness:** Similar to other brush-based tools.
   - **Range:** Specifies which tonal range to affect:
   - **Shadows:** Affects the darkest areas of the image.
   - **Midtones:** Affects the middle tones.
   - **Highlights:** Affects the lightest areas.
   - **Exposure:** Controls the strength of the effect. A lower exposure produces a more subtle effect.
   - **Protect Tones:** When checked, this option attempts to minimize clipping in the shadows and highlights and can help to prevent color shifts.

3. **Paint over the areas** you want to lighten or darken.

Tips for Using the Dodge and Burn Tools:
- **Use a low Exposure setting (e.g., 5-15%)** and build up the effect gradually with multiple strokes. This allows for more control and prevents overdoing it.
- **Use a soft brush** for a more natural-looking result.
- **Zoom in** to work on details.
- **Frequently switch between the Dodge and Burn tools** to maintain a balanced look.
- **Create a separate layer for dodging and burning** to work non-destructively. A common technique is to create a new layer filled with 50% gray and set the blending mode to Overlay or Soft Light.

8.9 The Sponge Tool: Adjusting Saturation

The Sponge Tool allows you to selectively increase or decrease the color saturation of an area.

How to Use the Sponge Tool:
1. **Select the Sponge Tool (O)** from the Tools Panel (it's grouped with the Dodge and Burn tools).
2. **Adjust the brush settings in the Options Bar:**
   - **Brush Size, Hardness:** Similar to other brush-based tools.
   - **Mode:**
     - **Desaturate:** Decreases saturation, moving colors towards gray.
     - **Saturate:** Increases saturation, making colors more vibrant.
   - **Flow:** Controls the strength of the effect.
   - **Vibrance:** When checked, this option attempts to prevent fully saturated colors from becoming clipped.

3. **Paint over the areas** where you want to adjust the saturation.

Tips for Using the Sponge Tool:
- **Use a low Flow setting** and build up the effect gradually.
- **Use a soft brush** for a more natural-looking result.
- **The Sponge Tool is useful for subtly adjusting the saturation of specific areas**, such as making the sky a bit more blue or desaturating distracting elements in the background.

8.10 Advanced Retouching with Frequency Separation

Frequency separation is a more advanced retouching technique that involves separating an image into high-frequency and low-frequency layers. This allows you to edit details (texture, blemishes) and color/tone independently, leading to more natural-looking results, especially in portrait retouching.

- **Low Frequency:** Contains the smooth tones, colors, and gradients of the image.
- **High Frequency:** Contains the fine details, such as skin texture, hair, and edges.

Basic Frequency Separation Steps:

1. **Duplicate the Background layer twice.** Name the lower layer "Low Frequency" and the upper layer "High Frequency."
2. **Blur the Low Frequency layer:** Select the "Low Frequency" layer and apply a **Gaussian Blur (Filter > Blur > Gaussian Blur)**. The radius should be large enough to blur out the fine details but not so large that it significantly alters the overall tones. A good starting point is around 4-8 pixels.
3. **Apply Image to the High Frequency layer:** Select the "High Frequency" layer and go to **Image > Apply Image**.
   - **Layer:** Choose the "Low Frequency" layer.
   - **Blending:** Subtract.
   - **Scale:** 2.
   - **Offset:** 128.
   - Click **OK**.
4. **Change the blending mode of the High Frequency layer to Linear Light.**

Retouching on the Separate Layers:

- **Low Frequency:** Use the **Clone Stamp Tool** (with a soft brush and low opacity, sampling from Current & Below), **Mixer Brush Tool**, or even the **Lasso Tool** with a large feather followed by another application of Gaussian Blur to smooth out uneven skin tones, remove shadows or highlights, and correct color inconsistencies. Since this layer contains no fine detail, you can be less precise.
- **High Frequency:** Use the **Healing Brush** or **Clone Stamp Tool** (with a small, soft brush and low opacity, sampling from Current Layer) to remove blemishes, wrinkles, stray hairs, and other imperfections. Work carefully to preserve the skin texture.

Advantages of Frequency Separation:

- **More Natural-Looking Results:** By separating detail from tone, you can avoid the "plastic" look that can result from over-retouching.
- **Greater Control:** You can independently adjust the smoothness of skin and the sharpness of details.
- **Flexibility:** You can always go back and readjust the blur on the Low Frequency layer or refine your edits on either layer.

Tips for Frequency Separation:

- **Start with a low blur radius** and gradually increase it if needed.
- **Don't overdo it.** Frequency separation is a powerful technique, but it's easy to go too far. Aim for subtle, natural-looking results.

- **Zoom in and out frequently** to check your progress at different magnification levels.
- **Practice makes perfect.** Frequency separation takes some practice to master, so don't be discouraged if your first attempts aren't perfect.

This concludes Chapter 8! You've now learned about a wide range of retouching tools and techniques, from the basic Red Eye Tool to the advanced frequency separation method. You're well-equipped to tackle a variety of retouching tasks and enhance your images with precision.

Color Correction and Adjustment

Color and tone are fundamental aspects of an image's overall impact and aesthetic appeal. Photoshop offers a robust set of tools for correcting and adjusting color and tone, allowing you to fix problems, enhance mood, and achieve your creative vision. This chapter will explore some of the most important adjustment tools, including histograms, Brightness/Contrast, Levels, Curves, Exposure, and Vibrance/Saturation.

9.1 Understanding Histograms: Analyzing Image Tones

A histogram is a graphical representation of the tonal distribution in an image. It shows the number of pixels at each brightness level, from pure black (0) on the left to pure white (255) on the right. Learning to read a histogram is essential for understanding and correcting the tonal balance of your images.

Opening the Histogram Panel:
Go to **Window > Histogram**.

Parts of a Histogram:
- **Horizontal Axis (X-Axis):** Represents the tonal range, from black (0) on the left to white (255) on the right.
- **Vertical Axis (Y-Axis):** Represents the number of pixels at each brightness level.
- **Shadows:** The left side of the histogram represents the darkest tones (shadows).
- **Midtones:** The middle of the histogram represents the midtones.
- **Highlights:** The right side of the histogram represents the brightest tones (highlights).

Interpreting Histograms:
- **Well-Balanced Image:** A well-balanced image typically has a histogram that's relatively evenly distributed across the tonal range, without large gaps or spikes.
- **Underexposed Image:** An underexposed image will have a histogram that's shifted to the left, with most of the pixels clustered in the shadow areas.

- **Overexposed Image:** An overexposed image will have a histogram that's shifted to the right, with most of the pixels clustered in the highlight areas.
- **Clipping:** When the histogram shows a sharp spike at either end (touching the edges of the graph), it indicates clipping.
    - **Shadow Clipping:** Loss of detail in the darkest areas, which are rendered as pure black.
    - **Highlight Clipping:** Loss of detail in the brightest areas, which are rendered as pure white.

- **Low Contrast:** A histogram that is bunched up in the middle and does not reach either end indicates an image that may lack contrast.
- **High Contrast:** A histogram with peaks at the ends and a dip in the middle indicates an image that may have high contrast.

Histogram Panel Options:
- **Channel:** You can view the histogram for the composite RGB channel or for individual color channels (Red, Green, Blue). This is helpful for diagnosing color casts or imbalances.
- **Source:** You can view the histogram for the entire image, a specific layer, or an adjustment layer.
- **Refresh:** The histogram may not update in real-time. The Cached Data Warning icon (a triangle with an exclamation point) will be shown if the histogram is generated from the cache. Click the **Uncached Refresh** button to update the histogram to the most accurate representation.
- **Statistics:** The panel will display information including the Mean, Standard Deviation, Median, Pixel Count, and more.

Using Histograms for Adjustments:
The histogram is a valuable tool for guiding your adjustments. By observing how your adjustments affect the histogram, you can make more informed decisions about how to improve the tonal balance of your image.

9.2 Brightness/Contrast: Adjusting Overall Tonality

Brightness/Contrast is one of the simplest adjustment tools in Photoshop. It allows you to adjust the overall brightness and contrast of an image.

Applying Brightness/Contrast:
- **As an Adjustment Layer (Recommended):**
    1. Go to **Layer > New Adjustment Layer > Brightness/Contrast**.
    2. Or, click the **Brightness/Contrast** icon in the **Adjustments** panel.

- **Directly to a Layer (Destructive):**
    - Go to **Image > Adjustments > Brightness/Contrast**. (This method is destructive, so it's generally not recommended.)

Brightness/Contrast Controls:

2. **Brightness:** Makes the image lighter or darker overall.
3. **Contrast:** Increases or decreases the difference between the light and dark areas of the image.
4. **Use Legacy:** This option uses the older, less sophisticated algorithm for Brightness/Contrast adjustments from previous Photoshop versions. Generally, you won't need to use this.
5. **Auto:** This uses AI to attempt automatic adjustment of brightness and contrast.

Tips for Using Brightness/Contrast:

1. **Use the adjustment layer method** for non-destructive editing.
2. **Watch the histogram** as you make adjustments to avoid clipping.
3. **Brightness/Contrast is a relatively blunt tool.** For more precise tonal control, use Levels or Curves.

9.3 Levels: Fine-Tuning Highlights, Midtones, and Shadows

Levels is a more powerful tool than Brightness/Contrast for adjusting the tonal range of an image. It allows you to control the brightness of the shadows, midtones, and highlights independently.

Applying Levels:

- **As an Adjustment Layer (Recommended):**
    - Go to **Layer > New Adjustment Layer > Levels**.
    - Or, click the **Levels** icon in the **Adjustments** panel.

- **Directly to a Layer (Destructive):**
    - Go to **Image > Adjustments > Levels**. (This method is destructive.)

Levels Dialog Box:

- **Histogram:** The Levels dialog box displays a histogram of the image's tonal distribution.
- **Input Levels:** The three sliders below the histogram control the input levels:
    - **Black Point Slider (Left):** Defines the darkest point in the image. Moving it to the right makes the shadows darker.
    - **Midtone Slider (Middle):** Adjusts the brightness of the midtones. Moving it to the left makes the midtones brighter, and moving it to the right makes them darker.
    - **White Point Slider (Right):** Defines the lightest point in the image. Moving it to the left makes the highlights brighter.

- **Output Levels:** The two sliders below the Input Levels control the output levels:
    - **Black Output Level (Left):** Lightens the darkest shadows by setting the darkest possible output value to a level above pure black (0).

- **White Output Level (Right):** Darkens the brightest highlights by setting the brightest possible output value to a level below pure white (255).
- **Eyedroppers:** The three eyedropper tools allow you to set the black point, gray point (midtone), and white point by clicking on specific areas of the image.
- **Auto:** This uses AI to attempt an automatic adjustment of levels.
- **Options:** This will open the Auto Color Correction Options dialog. Here, you can fine-tune how the Auto button will behave. You can also set target colors for shadows, midtones, and highlights.

Tips for Using Levels:

- **Adjust the black and white point sliders** to the edges of the histogram to expand the tonal range of the image and improve contrast, but watch for clipping.
- **Use the midtone slider** to fine-tune the overall brightness of the image.
- **Use the eyedropper tools** to set the black, gray, and white points based on specific areas of your image. This can be helpful for correcting color casts. For example, clicking on an area that should be neutral gray with the middle eyedropper will adjust the colors so that the area becomes gray.
- **Watch the histogram** as you make adjustments to avoid clipping and ensure a balanced tonal distribution.

9.4 Curves: Advanced Tonal Control

Curves is the most powerful and flexible tool for adjusting the tone and contrast of an image. It gives you precise control over the entire tonal range, allowing you to make very subtle or dramatic adjustments.

Applying Curves:

- **As an Adjustment Layer (Recommended):**
  - Go to **Layer > New Adjustment Layer > Curves**.
  - Or, click the **Curves** icon in the **Adjustments** panel.

- **Directly to a Layer (Destructive):**
  - Go to **Image > Adjustments > Curves**. (This method is destructive.)

Curves Dialog Box:

- **The Curve:** The diagonal line represents the tonal range of the image. The horizontal axis (bottom) represents the input levels (original brightness values), and the vertical axis (left) represents the output levels (new brightness values).
- **Adding Points:** Click on the curve to add control points.
- **Adjusting Points:** Drag control points up to lighten the corresponding tones and down to darken them.
- **Input/Output Values:** As you move a point, you'll see its input and output values displayed below the curve. You can also enter specific values numerically.
- **Curve Display Options:** You can display the curve as Light (0-255) or Pigment/Ink % by clicking the double-arrow above the top-right of the curve graph.
- **Channel:** By default, you're adjusting the composite RGB curve, which affects all three color channels. You can also select individual color channels (Red, Green, Blue) from the drop-down menu to make color-specific adjustments.
- **Pencil Tool:** The pencil tool allows you to draw a freehand curve. This is generally less precise than using control points.
- **Smooth:** This button smooths out a curve that you drew with the Pencil tool.
- **Auto:** This uses AI to attempt an automatic adjustment of the curve.
- **Eyedroppers:** Similar to Levels, you can use the eyedropper tools to set the black, gray, and white points by clicking on specific areas of the image.
- **Show Clipping:** This checkbox will allow you to visualize areas of your image that are clipping.
- **Intersection Line:** This displays a vertical line that shows you the affected tones as you move your mouse across the curve.

Common Curve Adjustments:

- **S-Curve:** A gentle S-shaped curve increases contrast by making the highlights brighter and the shadows darker.
- **Inverted S-Curve:** An inverted S-curve decreases contrast by making the highlights darker and the shadows lighter.
- **Lifting the Black Point:** Slightly raising the bottom-left point of the curve can create a "faded" or "matte" look by lifting the shadows.

Tips for Using Curves:
- **Start with small adjustments.** It's easy to overdo it with Curves.
- **Add a few control points** and adjust them gradually.
- **Use the histogram** as a guide.
- **Experiment with different curve shapes** to see how they affect the image.
- **Use Curves in conjunction with other adjustment layers** for even greater control.

9.5 Exposure: Correcting Overexposed and Underexposed Images

The Exposure adjustment is primarily designed to correct exposure problems, making images that are too dark (underexposed) or too bright (overexposed) appear more balanced.

Applying Exposure:
- **As an Adjustment Layer (Recommended):**
    1. Go to **Layer > New Adjustment Layer > Exposure**.
    2. Or, click the **Exposure** icon in the **Adjustments** panel.

- **Directly to a Layer (Destructive):**
    1. Go to **Image > Adjustments > Exposure**. (This method is destructive.)

Exposure Controls:
- **Exposure:** Adjusts the overall brightness of the image, primarily affecting the highlights. Positive values increase exposure (brighten), while negative values decrease exposure (darken). This slider has the greatest effect on highlights.
- **Offset:** Adjusts the darkness of the shadows. Positive values lighten the shadows, while negative values darken them. This slider has the greatest effect on shadows. Use this slider with caution, as it can make the image look "flat" or "muddy" if overused.
- **Gamma Correction:** Adjusts the brightness of the midtones. It's similar to the midtone slider in Levels but uses a slightly different algorithm. Positive values will lighten midtones, while negative values will darken them.

Tips for Using Exposure:
- **Use it to correct overall exposure problems.** If your image is simply too dark or too bright, the Exposure adjustment can often fix it.
- **Watch the histogram** to avoid clipping highlights or shadows.
- **For more advanced tonal adjustments, use Levels or Curves.**

9.6 Vibrance and Saturation: Enhancing Colors

Vibrance and Saturation are used to adjust the intensity of colors in an image.

Applying Vibrance and Saturation:
- **As an Adjustment Layer (Recommended):**

1. Go to **Layer > New Adjustment Layer > Vibrance**.
2. Or, click the **Vibrance** icon in the **Adjustments** panel.

- **Directly to a Layer (Destructive):**
    1. Go to **Image > Adjustments > Vibrance**. (This method is destructive.)

Vibrance and Saturation Controls:
- **Vibrance:** Increases the intensity of *less saturated* colors while having a lesser effect on *already saturated* colors. It also helps to prevent skin tones from becoming oversaturated. This makes it a more subtle and often preferred adjustment than Saturation.
- **Saturation:** Increases the intensity of *all* colors equally. Be careful with this slider, as it can easily make an image look unnatural if overused.

Tips for Using Vibrance and Saturation:
- **Use Vibrance for a more natural-looking boost in color intensity.**
- **Use Saturation sparingly.**
- **Watch for color clipping.** Oversaturating colors can cause them to lose detail and appear "blocky." You can use the Gamut Warning to identify areas where this is occurring.

9.7 Hue/Saturation: Shifting and Modifying Colors

Hue/Saturation is a powerful tool for adjusting the overall color scheme of an image or targeting specific color ranges. It allows you to change the hue (color), saturation (intensity), and lightness (brightness) of colors.

Applying Hue/Saturation:
- **As an Adjustment Layer (Recommended):**
    1. Go to **Layer > New Adjustment Layer > Hue/Saturation**.
    2. Or, click the **Hue/Saturation** icon in the **Adjustments** panel.

- **Directly to a Layer (Destructive):**
    1. Go to **Image > Adjustments > Hue/Saturation**. (This method is destructive.)

Hue/Saturation Controls:
- **Edit:**
    1. **Master:** Adjusts all colors in the image simultaneously.
    2. **Specific Color Ranges (Reds, Yellows, Greens, Cyans, Blues, Magentas):** Allows you to target specific color ranges for adjustment.
    3. **Add to Sample, Subtract from Sample:** The eyedropper tools allow you to further refine your color selection.

4. **Color Bar:** This represents the entire spectrum of hues. The lower color bar shows the currently selected hues. The upper color bar shows how those hues will be affected by the adjustment.

- **Hue:** Shifts the colors along the color wheel.
- **Saturation:** Increases or decreases the intensity of colors.
- **Lightness:** Makes colors lighter or darker.
- **Colorize:** Converts the image to a monotone color, allowing you to choose a single hue and adjust its saturation and lightness. This is useful for creating sepia or other tinted effects.

Tips for Using Hue/Saturation:

- **Use the "On-Image" adjustment tool:** This allows you to click and drag directly on the image to adjust the hue or saturation of a specific color. Click the icon that looks like a hand with arrows pointing left and right.
- **Target specific color ranges** for more precise adjustments.
- **Use Hue/Saturation in conjunction with layer masks** to apply color changes selectively to certain areas of an image.
- **Use the Colorize option** to create interesting monotone or duotone effects.

9.8 Color Balance: Correcting Color Casts

Color Balance is used to correct unwanted color casts in an image or to add creative color effects. It allows you to adjust the balance of colors in the shadows, midtones, and highlights independently.

Applying Color Balance:

- **As an Adjustment Layer (Recommended):**
  1. Go to **Layer > New Adjustment Layer > Color Balance**.
  2. Or, click the **Color Balance** icon in the **Adjustments** panel.

- **Directly to a Layer (Destructive):**
  1. Go to **Image > Adjustments > Color Balance**. (This method is destructive.)

Color Balance Controls:

- **Tone Balance:** Choose whether to adjust the **Shadows**, **Midtones**, or **Highlights**.
- **Color Levels:** Three sliders for each tone range allow you to add or subtract color:
  - **Cyan/Red**
  - **Magenta/Green**
  - **Yellow/Blue**
- **Preserve Luminosity:** When checked, this option maintains the overall brightness of the image while you adjust the colors. It is generally recommended to keep this checked.

Tips for Using Color Balance:

- **Identify the color cast:** Determine which color is dominant in the image (e.g., too much yellow, too much blue).
- **Adjust the sliders in the opposite direction of the color cast.** For example, if the image is too yellow, move the Yellow/Blue slider towards blue.
- **Start with the midtones,** then fine-tune the shadows and highlights.
- **Use Color Balance subtly** for natural-looking corrections.

9.9 Black & White: Creating Stunning Monochrome Images

The Black & White adjustment offers a sophisticated way to convert color images to grayscale, giving you a lot of control over how different colors are translated into shades of gray.

Applying Black & White:

- **As an Adjustment Layer (Recommended):**
    1. Go to **Layer > New Adjustment Layer > Black & White**.
    2. Or, click the **Black & White** icon in the **Adjustments** panel.

- **Directly to a Layer (Destructive):**
    1. Go to **Image > Adjustments > Black & White**. (This method is destructive.)

Black & White Controls:

- **Presets:** A variety of preset options (e.g., "Infrared," "High Contrast Red Filter") that simulate the look of traditional black and white film and filters.
- **Color Sliders (Reds, Yellows, Greens, Cyans, Blues, Magentas):** These sliders control the brightness of areas in the original image that correspond to those colors. For example, moving the Reds slider to the right will make areas that were originally red appear brighter in the black and white version.
- **Auto:** Uses AI to attempt an automatic adjustment of the sliders.
- **Tint:** Adds a color tint to the black and white image (e.g., sepia, selenium).

Tips for Using Black & White:
- **Experiment with the color sliders** to find the best tonal balance for your image.
- **Use the "On-Image" adjustment tool:** Similar to Hue/Saturation, you can click and drag directly on the image to adjust the brightness of specific colors.
- **Consider the mood and style** you want to achieve. Different slider combinations can create dramatically different results.

9.10 Photo Filter: Adding Color Tints and Effects

Photo Filter simulates the effect of placing a colored filter in front of your camera lens. It's a quick way to add color tints or correct the overall color temperature of an image.

Applying Photo Filter:
- **As an Adjustment Layer (Recommended):**
  1. Go to **Layer > New Adjustment Layer > Photo Filter**.
  2. Or, click the **Photo Filter** icon in the **Adjustments** panel.
- **Directly to a Layer (Destructive):**
  1. Go to **Image > Adjustments > Photo Filter**. (This method is destructive.)

Photo Filter Controls:
- **Filter:** Choose from a variety of preset filter colors (e.g., "Warming Filter (85)," "Cooling Filter (80)," "Sepia").
- **Color:** Select a custom color for the filter.
- **Density:** Controls the strength of the filter effect.
- **Preserve Luminosity:** When checked, this option maintains the overall brightness of the image.

Tips for Using Photo Filter:
- **Use Warming Filters** to add warmth to an image.
- **Use Cooling Filters** to cool down an image or correct for overly warm lighting.
- **Use the Density slider** to fine-tune the intensity of the effect.

9.11 Channel Mixer: Advanced Color Adjustments

The Channel Mixer allows you to create custom color adjustments by mixing the color channels of an image. It's a powerful tool for advanced color correction and creative effects, but it can be a bit more complex to use than other adjustment tools.

Applying Channel Mixer:
- **As an Adjustment Layer (Recommended):**
  1. Go to **Layer > New Adjustment Layer > Channel Mixer**.
  2. Or, click the **Channel Mixer** icon in the **Adjustments** panel.
- **Directly to a Layer (Destructive):**

1. Go to **Image > Adjustments > Channel Mixer**. (This method is destructive.)

Channel Mixer Controls:
- **Output Channel:** Select the color channel you want to modify (Red, Green, or Blue).
- **Source Channels:** The sliders for each source channel (Red, Green, Blue) control how much of that channel's information is mixed into the output channel.
- **Constant:** Adds a constant amount of black or white to the output channel, effectively making it darker or lighter.
- **Monochrome:** Converts the image to grayscale, but unlike a simple desaturation, it allows you to control how each color channel contributes to the brightness of the grayscale image, similar to the Black & White adjustment.

Tips for Using Channel Mixer:
- **For subtle color adjustments, make small changes to the Source Channel sliders.**
- **To avoid color shifts when adjusting individual channels, make sure the total percentage of the three source channels adds up to 100%.**
- **Use the Monochrome option** for advanced black and white conversions.

9.12 Invert, Posterize, Threshold, Gradient Map, Selective Color

These are additional adjustment tools that can be useful for specific tasks or creative effects:

- **Invert:** Inverts the colors of an image, like a photographic negative. (**Image > Adjustments > Invert** or **Layer > New Adjustment Layer > Invert**)
- **Posterize:** Reduces the number of tonal levels in an image, creating a flat, poster-like effect. (**Image > Adjustments > Posterize** or **Layer > New Adjustment Layer > Posterize**)
- **Threshold:** Converts an image to pure black and white, with no shades of gray. You can adjust the threshold level to control which pixels are converted to black and which to white. (**Image > Adjustments > Threshold** or **Layer > New Adjustment Layer > Threshold**)
- **Gradient Map:** Maps the tones of an image to a specified gradient. This can be used to create interesting color effects or to colorize a grayscale image. (**Image > Adjustments > Gradient Map** or **Layer > New Adjustment Layer > Gradient Map**)
- **Selective Color:** Allows you to selectively adjust the amount of cyan, magenta, yellow, and black in specific color ranges (Reds, Yellows, Greens, etc.) or in the highlights, midtones, or shadows. This is often used for fine-tuning colors in print workflows, but it can also be used creatively. (**Image > Adjustments > Selective Color** or **Layer > New Adjustment Layer > Selective Color**)

These three adjustment commands offer unique ways to manipulate colors and tones in your images:

- **Match Color:**
  - **Purpose:** Matches the color and luminosity of one image (the source) to another image (the target) or between layers or selections within the same image. This can be useful for creating consistency between multiple images or for stylizing an image based on the colors of another.

  - **How to Use:**
    1. Open both the source and target images.
    2. Select the target image, layer, or selection where you want to apply the color matching.
    3. Go to **Image > Adjustments > Match Color**.
    4. In the Match Color dialog box:
- **Source:** Choose the source image from the drop-down menu.
- **Layer:** If the source image has multiple layers, choose the layer you want to use as the source.
- **Image Statistics:**
  - **Use Selection in Source to Calculate Colors:** If the source image has a selection, check this option to use only the selected area for color matching.
  - **Use Selection in Target to Calculate Adjustment:** If the target image has a selection, check this option to apply the color matching only to the selected area.
  - **Ignore Selection When Applying Adjustment:** Check this if you do not want to constrain your adjustment to a selection within your target image.
  - **Target:** This section shows the target image and layer.
- **Adjustment:**
  - **Luminance:** Adjusts the brightness of the matched colors.
  - **Color Intensity:** Adjusts the saturation of the matched colors.
  - **Fade:** Allows you to blend between the original colors of the target image and the matched colors.
  - **Neutralize:** Attempts to remove any color casts in the matched colors.
  - Click **OK** to apply the color matching.

- **Replace Color:**
  - **Purpose:** Allows you to select a specific color range in an image and replace it with another color. It's similar to using the Hue/Saturation adjustment, but it provides a different interface for selecting and modifying colors.
  - **How to Use:**
    1. Go to **Image > Adjustments > Replace Color**.
    2. In the Replace Color dialog box:
- **Selection:** Use the eyedropper tools to select the color range you want to replace. The white areas in the preview represent the selected pixels.
- **Add to Sample:** Use the plus eyedropper to add more colors to the selection.

- **Subtract from Sample:** Use the minus eyedropper to remove colors from the selection.
- **Fuzziness:** Controls the tolerance of the color selection, similar to the Tolerance setting for the Magic Wand tool.
- **Replacement:**
  - **Hue:** Shifts the hue of the selected colors.
  - **Saturation:** Adjusts the saturation of the selected colors.
  - **Lightness:** Adjusts the lightness of the selected colors.
  - Click **OK** to apply the color replacement.

- **Equalize:**
  - **Purpose:** Redistributes the brightness values of pixels in an image so that they more evenly represent the entire range of brightness levels. This can be useful for revealing details in images that are very dark or very light, but it often produces an unrealistic or stylized look.
  o **How to Use:**
  1. Go to **Image > Adjustments > Equalize**.
  2. In the Equalize dialog box, choose whether to equalize based on:
     - **Entire Image Based on Area:** Uses the entire image to calculate the equalization.
     - **Selected Area Only:** Uses only the selected area to calculate the equalization.
       1. Click **OK** to apply the equalization.

9.14 HDR Toning

HDR (High Dynamic Range) Toning is designed to simulate the look of high dynamic range images, which have a wider range of brightness levels than standard images. While true HDR images are created by combining multiple exposures, HDR Toning allows you to create an HDR-like effect from a single image.

How to Use HDR Toning:
- Go to **Image > Adjustments > HDR Toning**.
- In the HDR Toning dialog box, you'll find a variety of settings to adjust:

o **Method:**
   2. **Exposure and Gamma:** Allows you to adjust exposure and gamma correction.
   3. **Highlight Compression:** Compresses the highlights to bring out more detail in the brightest areas.
   4. **Equalize Histogram:** Similar to the Equalize command, but with more control over the result.
   5. **Local Adaptation:** Provides the most control and flexibility, allowing you to adjust various parameters like edge glow, tone, and detail.
o **Edge Glow:** Adjusts the appearance of edges, making them glow or appear more defined.
o **Tone and Detail:** Fine-tunes the overall tonal balance and the level of detail.
o **Advanced:** Provides access to shadow, highlight, vibrance, and saturation controls.
o **Toning Curve and Histogram:** Allows for further adjustments using a curves-like interface.

Tips for Using HDR Toning:
1. **Start with the Local Adaptation method** for the most control.
2. **Experiment with the different settings** to see how they affect the image.
3. **HDR Toning can easily be overdone**, so use it with restraint if you're aiming for a natural look.

9.15 Shadows/Highlights

The Shadows/Highlights adjustment is specifically designed to improve the detail in the shadow and highlight areas of an image. It's particularly useful for images with high contrast or backlit scenes where the shadows are too dark or the highlights are too bright.

How to Use Shadows/Highlights:
1. Go to **Image > Adjustments > Shadows/Highlights**.
2. In the Shadows/Highlights dialog box:

o **Shadows:**
   1. **Amount:** Controls the amount of lightening applied to the shadows.

2. **Tone:** Controls the range of shadows that are affected. Lower values affect a wider range of shadows, while higher values target only the darkest shadows.
3. **Radius:** Determines the size of the area around each pixel that is analyzed when making the adjustment. Larger values produce a more gradual and natural-looking adjustment.

- **Highlights:**
    1. **Amount:** Controls the amount of darkening applied to the highlights.
    2. **Tone:** Controls the range of highlights that are affected.
    3. **Radius:** Similar to the Radius setting for Shadows.
- **Adjustments:**
    1. **Color Correction:** Adjusts the color saturation in the adjusted areas.
    2. **Midtone Contrast:** Increases or decreases the contrast in the midtones.
    3. **Black Clip/White Clip:** Specifies how much to clip the shadows and highlights to pure black or white.

Tips for Using Shadows/Highlights:

2. **Start with small adjustments** to the Amount sliders.
3. **Check the "Show More Options" box** to reveal the advanced controls.
4. **Use the Radius sliders** to fine-tune the blending and create a more natural look.

Photoshop has incorporated AI-powered features to assist with automatic color and tonal adjustments. While these tools may not always produce perfect results, they can be a good starting point, especially for batch processing or quick fixes.

AI-Powered Adjustment Options:

1. **Auto Tone:** (**Image > Auto Tone** or **Shift+Ctrl+L / Shift+Cmd+L**) Automatically adjusts the overall tonal range of the image.
2. **Auto Contrast:** (**Image > Auto Contrast**) Automatically adjusts the contrast of the image.
3. **Auto Color:** (**Image > Auto Color** or **Shift+Ctrl+B / Shift+Cmd+B**) Automatically adjusts the color balance of the image.
4. **Auto Buttons in Adjustment Layers:** Many adjustment layer dialog boxes (e.g., Levels, Curves, Brightness/Contrast) have an **Auto** button that uses AI to suggest automatic adjustments.

How AI Can Help:

1. **Speeding Up Workflow:** AI can quickly analyze an image and suggest adjustments, saving you time.
2. **Batch Processing:** AI-powered adjustments can be applied to multiple images automatically using actions or batch processing.
3. **Starting Point for Manual Adjustments:** Even if the automatic adjustments aren't perfect, they can provide a good starting point for further manual refinements.

Limitations of AI:

1. **Artistic Interpretation:** AI lacks the artistic judgment of a human editor. It may not always make the best choices for the mood or style you're trying to achieve.
2. **Complex Images:** AI may struggle with complex images or images with unusual lighting or color conditions.
3. **Subtlety:** AI adjustments can sometimes be too heavy-handed.

Best Practices for Using AI:

1. **Use AI as a starting point, not a final solution.** Always review the results and make manual adjustments as needed.
2. **Experiment with different AI options** to see which one works best for a particular image.
3. **Combine AI with your own knowledge and skills** to achieve the best results.

This completes Chapter 9! You've now explored a comprehensive range of color and tonal adjustment tools and techniques in Photoshop, from the basics of histograms and Brightness/Contrast to more advanced tools like Curves, Channel Mixer, and HDR Toning. You've also learned about AI-powered automatic adjustments and how to use them effectively. With

this knowledge, you're well-equipped to enhance the color, tone, and overall impact of your images. In the next chapter, we'll move on to the exciting world of filters, where you'll discover a vast array of creative possibilities for transforming and stylizing your images.

Filters and Effects

Filters are one of the most exciting and versatile features in Photoshop. They allow you to transform your images in countless ways, from subtle enhancements to dramatic special effects. You can use filters to correct imperfections, stylize your images, create artistic looks, and much more. This chapter will provide an overview of Photoshop's Filter Gallery, explain how to use Smart Filters for non-destructive editing, and explore some of the most commonly used filter categories: Blur, Sharpen, and Noise.

10.1 An Overview of Photoshop's Filter Gallery

The Filter Gallery is a central hub for accessing and applying a wide range of Photoshop filters. It provides a visual preview of each filter's effect and allows you to combine multiple filters to create unique looks.

Accessing the Filter Gallery:
- Go to **Filter > Filter Gallery**.

Navigating the Filter Gallery:
- **Filter Categories:** The left side of the Filter Gallery window displays a list of filter categories (e.g., Artistic, Brush Strokes, Distort, Sketch, Stylize, Texture).
- **Filter Thumbnails:** When you select a category, thumbnails of the filters within that category appear.
- **Preview Window:** The large preview window shows you how the selected filter will affect your image. You can zoom in and out using the plus and minus buttons in the bottom-left corner.
- **Filter Settings:** The right side of the window displays the settings for the selected filter. Each filter has its own unique set of controls.
- **Adding Multiple Filters:** You can apply multiple filters by clicking the **New effect layer** icon at the bottom of the Filter Settings pane. This creates a stack of filters, similar to a layer stack. You can reorder the filters in the stack by dragging them up or down.
- **Showing and Hiding Filters:** Click the eye icon next to a filter in the stack to show or hide its effect.
- **Deleting Filters:** Click on a filter in the stack and then click the **Delete effect layer** icon (trash can).

Filter Categories:
Here's a brief overview of the filter categories available in the Filter Gallery:
- **Artistic:** Simulate traditional art media, such as watercolor, paint daubs, and colored pencil.
- **Brush Strokes:** Apply various brush stroke effects, such as angled strokes, crosshatch, and spatter.
- **Distort:** Distort the image in various ways, such as with ripples, waves, and glass distortion.

- **Sketch:** Create sketch-like effects using different techniques, such as charcoal, conte crayon, and graphic pen.
- **Stylize:** Apply a variety of stylistic effects, such as glowing edges, extruded blocks, and tiles.
- **Texture:** Add texture to the image, such as craquelure, grain, and mosaic tiles.
- **Other:** The Filter Gallery contains only a subset of Photoshop's total filters. Many more are found under the Filter menu.

Important Note: Not all filters are available in the Filter Gallery. Some, like the **Camera Raw Filter**, **Liquify**, and **Vanishing Point**, have their own separate interfaces.

10.2 Applying Filters Non-Destructively with Smart Filters

As you learned in Chapter 7, Smart Filters are a powerful way to apply filters non-destructively, allowing you to edit the filter settings at any time without permanently altering the original image data.

How to Apply Smart Filters:
1. **Convert the layer to a Smart Object:** Before applying a filter, convert the layer you want to affect into a Smart Object. You can do this by right-clicking (Windows) or Control-clicking (macOS) on the layer in the Layers Panel and choosing **Convert to Smart Object**.
2. **Apply the filter:** Go to **Filter** in the Menu Bar and choose the desired filter. If you're using the Filter Gallery, click **OK** to apply the filter(s).

What Happens:
- The filter will be applied as a Smart Filter, appearing as a separate, editable item beneath the Smart Object layer in the Layers Panel.
- You'll see a small icon next to the Smart Object's thumbnail indicating that it has Smart Filters applied.

Editing Smart Filters:
- **Double-click** the name of the Smart Filter in the Layers Panel to reopen its settings dialog and make adjustments.
- **Change the Blending Mode or Opacity:** Click the small icon with two sliders next to the filter's name in the Layers Panel.
- **Hide or Show:** Click the eye icon next to the Smart Filter to temporarily hide or show its effect.
- **Reorder:** Drag and drop Smart Filters in the Layers Panel to change their order of application.
- **Delete:** Drag the Smart Filter to the trash can icon at the bottom of the Layers Panel.
- **Masking Smart Filters:**
- Each Smart Filter has a mask associated with it (the white thumbnail next to the filter's name).

- You can paint on the mask with black to hide the filter's effect in specific areas, white to reveal it, or shades of gray to partially apply the effect.

Benefits of Smart Filters:

- **Flexibility:** You can change filter settings at any time without degrading image quality.
- **Experimentation:** Try out different filter combinations and settings without committing to them permanently.
- **Non-Destructive Workflow:** Preserve the original image data and maintain a flexible editing process.

10.3 Blur Filters: Gaussian Blur, Motion Blur, Radial Blur, and More

Blur filters are used to soften images, reduce noise, create a sense of motion, or simulate a shallow depth of field. Here are some of the most commonly used blur filters:

- **Gaussian Blur: (Filter > Blur > Gaussian Blur)**
  - Applies a uniform blur based on a Gaussian curve, which produces a natural-looking softening effect.
  - **Radius:** Controls the amount of blur. A higher radius creates a stronger blur.
- **Motion Blur: (Filter > Blur > Motion Blur)**
  - Simulates the blur that results from moving an object or the camera during exposure.
  - **Angle:** Sets the direction of the motion.
  - **Distance:** Controls the amount of blur, simulating the speed of motion.
- **Radial Blur: (Filter > Blur > Radial Blur)**
  - Creates a blur that radiates outward from a central point, either spinning or zooming.
  - **Amount:** Controls the intensity of the blur.
  - **Method:**
    - **Spin:** Creates a circular blur.
    - **Zoom:** Creates a blur that radiates outward from the center.
  - **Quality:** Higher quality settings produce smoother results but take longer to render.
- **Box Blur:** This filter blurs an image based on the average color value of neighboring pixels.
- **Shape Blur:** This allows you to blur an image using a specified shape as a kernel.
- **Surface Blur:** This blurs an image while attempting to preserve edges.
- **Lens Blur:** This attempts to simulate the bokeh produced by a camera lens.
- **Smart Blur:** This gives you more fine-tuned control over how the blur is applied, allowing you to set a radius, threshold, and quality.

Other Blur Filters:

Photoshop offers other specialized blur filters under the **Filter > Blur** and **Filter > Blur Gallery** menus, including:

- **Field Blur:** Allows you to create gradual changes in blur by placing multiple pins on the image, each with a different blur setting.
- **Iris Blur:** Simulates a shallow depth-of-field effect, keeping a specific area in focus while blurring the rest.
- **Tilt-Shift:** Simulates the effect of a tilt-shift lens, which is often used to make real-life scenes look like miniature models.
- **Path Blur:** This creates a blur effect that follows a user-defined path.
- **Spin Blur:** This creates a circular blur effect that can be customized with various parameters.

Tips for Using Blur Filters:

- **Use Smart Filters** to apply blur non-destructively.
- **Use layer masks or Smart Filter masks** to selectively apply blur to specific areas of an image.
- **Combine different blur filters** to create unique effects.
- **Consider using blur filters in conjunction with other adjustments**, such as Levels or Curves, to enhance the overall effect.

10.4 Sharpen Filters: Unsharp Mask, Smart Sharpen, and More

Sharpen filters are used to enhance the definition of edges in an image, making it appear crisper and more focused. However, it's important to use sharpening with restraint, as over-sharpening can introduce unwanted artifacts and noise.

- **Unsharp Mask: (Filter > Sharpen > Unsharp Mask)**
  - Despite its name, Unsharp Mask is a sharpening filter. It works by increasing the contrast along edges in the image.
  - **Amount:** Controls the intensity of the sharpening effect.
  - **Radius:** Determines the width of the edges that are sharpened. A smaller radius affects only the finest details, while a larger radius affects broader areas.
  - **Threshold:** Specifies the minimum brightness difference between adjacent pixels that should be considered an edge and sharpened. Higher threshold values prevent the sharpening of subtle details and can help to avoid over-sharpening.

- **Smart Sharpen: (Filter > Sharpen > Smart Sharpen)**
  - Offers more advanced controls than Unsharp Mask, including the ability to adjust sharpening in the shadows and highlights independently.
  - **Amount:** Controls the overall strength of the sharpening.
  - **Radius:** Similar to Unsharp Mask, this determines the width of the edges to be sharpened.

- o **Reduce Noise:** Attempts to minimize noise that can be introduced by sharpening.
- o **Remove:** Allows you to choose the algorithm used to sharpen the image: Gaussian Blur, Lens Blur, or Motion Blur. This is useful for correcting specific types of blur.
- o **Shadow/Highlight:** These tabs allow for fine-tuning of the sharpening effect in the shadows and highlights, respectively.

Other Sharpen Filters:
- **Sharpen:** Applies a basic sharpening effect.
- **Sharpen Edges:** Sharpens only the edges in the image, leaving the smoother areas untouched.
- **Sharpen More:** Applies a stronger sharpening effect than the basic Sharpen filter.
- **Shake Reduction:** This filter attempts to reduce blur caused by camera shake.

Tips for Using Sharpen Filters:
- **Less is more.** It's easy to over-sharpen an image, which can make it look unnatural and grainy.
- **Use a low Radius** setting for fine details and a higher Radius for broader sharpening.
- **Use the Threshold** setting in Unsharp Mask to avoid sharpening noise.
- **Zoom in to 100%** to accurately assess the sharpening effect.
- **Apply sharpening as one of the last steps** in your editing workflow.

10.5 Noise Filters: Add Noise, Reduce Noise, and More

Noise filters are used to either add or remove noise from an image. Noise is often characterized by small, random variations in pixel color or brightness, giving the image a grainy appearance.

- **Add Noise: (Filter > Noise > Add Noise)**
  - o Adds random noise to an image, which can be used for artistic effects or to create a more "film-like" look.
  - o **Amount:** Controls the intensity of the noise.
  - o **Distribution:**
    - **Uniform:** Creates a more uniform noise pattern.
    - **Gaussian:** Creates a more natural-looking noise pattern based on a Gaussian distribution.
  - o **Monochromatic:** Adds grayscale noise instead of color noise.
- **Reduce Noise: (Filter > Noise > Reduce Noise)**
  - o Attempts to reduce noise in an image while preserving detail.
  - o **Strength:** Controls the overall amount of noise reduction.

- **Preserve Details:** Attempts to retain edge sharpness while reducing noise.
- **Reduce Color Noise:** Specifically targets color noise, which often appears as random colored speckles.
- **Sharpen Details:** Applies a degree of sharpening to compensate for any softening caused by noise reduction.
- **Remove JPEG Artifact:** This option can help to reduce artifacts caused by JPEG compression.

Other Noise Filters:

- **Despeckle:** Reduces noise by detecting and blurring edges.
- **Dust & Scratches:** Helps to remove dust, scratches, and other small imperfections.
- **Median:** Reduces noise by replacing each pixel with the median color value of the surrounding pixels.

Tips for Using Noise Filters:

- **Use the Reduce Noise filter with caution**, as it can soften the image and reduce detail if overused.
- **Zoom in to 100%** to accurately assess the noise and the effects of the filter.
- **Experiment with different settings** to find the best balance between noise reduction and detail preservation.
- **Consider using the Camera Raw Filter** for noise reduction, as it offers more advanced controls.

10.6 Stylize Filters: Find Edges, Emboss, Wind, and More

Stylize filters create a variety of artistic and special effects by modifying the pixels in an image based on different algorithms. They can be used to add texture, create edge effects, simulate hand-drawn looks, and more.

Here are some notable Stylize filters:

- **Find Edges: (Filter > Stylize > Find Edges)**
  - Detects and outlines the edges in an image, creating a line drawing effect.
- **Glowing Edges:** Similar to Find Edges, but it produces thicker, glowing lines.
- **Emboss: (Filter > Stylize > Emboss)**
  - Creates a 3D embossed effect by raising or lowering areas of the image based on their brightness and adding highlights and shadows.
  - **Angle:** Sets the direction of the light source.
  - **Height:** Controls the apparent height of the embossing.
  - **Amount:** Adjusts the intensity of the effect.
- **Extrude:** This creates a 3D effect by extruding the image into blocks or pyramids.
- **Tiles:** This divides the image into a grid of tiles and then shifts them randomly.
- **Wind: (Filter > Stylize > Wind)**

- Simulates the effect of wind blowing across the image, creating horizontal streaks.
- **Method:**
  - **Wind:** Creates fine lines.
  - **Blast:** Creates thicker, more pronounced streaks.
  - **Stagger:** Creates a more randomized, staggered effect.
- **Direction:** Sets the direction from which the wind is blowing (Right or Left).
- **Diffuse:** This filter diffuses the colors in an image by shifting pixels randomly.
- **Solarize:** This creates a partially negative effect, similar to what can happen when exposing photographic film to light during development.

Tips for Using Stylize Filters:
- **Experiment with different filters and settings** to discover the wide range of effects they can produce.
- **Combine Stylize filters with other filters and adjustments** to create unique looks.
- **Use Smart Filters** to apply Stylize filters non-destructively.
- **Consider using layer masks** to selectively apply the effects to specific areas of your image.

10.7 Distort Filters: Ripple, Wave, Twirl, and More

Distort filters geometrically distort an image, creating a variety of warping, twisting, and rippling effects.

Here are some commonly used Distort filters:

- **Ripple: (Filter > Distort > Ripple)**
  - Creates a series of concentric ripples, like the surface of water when a pebble is dropped in.
  - **Amount:** Controls the intensity of the ripples.
  - **Size:** Sets the size of the ripples (Small, Medium, or Large).
- **Wave: (Filter > Distort > Wave)**
  - Creates a series of undulating waves across the image.
  - **Number of Generators:** Controls the number of wave generators. More generators create a more complex wave pattern.
  - **Wavelength:** Sets the distance between wave crests.
  - **Amplitude:** Controls the height of the waves.
  - **Scale:** Adjusts the horizontal and vertical scale of the waves.
  - **Type:**
    - **Sine:** Creates smooth, rolling waves.
    - **Triangle:** Creates more angular waves.
    - **Square:** Creates square-shaped waves.
  - **Undefined Areas:** Determines how the filter handles areas that extend beyond the original image boundaries: Wrap Around or Repeat Edge Pixels.
- **Twirl: (Filter > Distort > Twirl)**
  - Rotates the image around its center, creating a swirling effect.
  - **Angle:** Controls the amount of rotation.
- **ZigZag:** This filter creates a series of zigzags or ripples emanating from the center of the image or selection.
- **Polar Coordinates:** This filter converts an image from its rectangular coordinates to polar coordinates, or vice versa.
- **Pinch:** This filter squeezes the image inward towards the center or pushes it outward.
- **Shear:** This filter distorts the image along a user-defined curve.
- **Spherize:** This filter creates a spherical distortion, making the image appear as if it were wrapped around a sphere.
- **Displace:** This filter uses a displacement map (another image) to distort the image.
- **Diffuse Glow:** This filter adds a glow to the lighter areas of an image and diffuses the colors.

Tips for Using Distort Filters:
- **Use Smart Filters** for non-destructive editing.
- **Combine Distort filters with layer masks** to apply the effects selectively.

- **Experiment with different settings** to achieve the desired effect. Some Distort filters have many parameters that can create a wide range of variations.
- **Consider using Distort filters on separate layers or Smart Objects** so you can easily adjust the effect without affecting the original image.

10.8 Render Filters: Clouds, Fibers, Lens Flare, Lighting Effects

Render filters generate new image content or add effects that simulate real-world phenomena like clouds, lens flares, and lighting.

- **Clouds: (Filter > Render > Clouds)**
  - Generates a random cloud pattern using the current foreground and background colors.
  - **Tip:** Hold down **Alt (Windows) / Option (macOS)** while selecting the Clouds filter to create a more contrasting cloud pattern.
- **Fibers: (Filter > Render > Fibers)**
  - Creates a texture that resembles woven fibers or strands of hair.
  - **Variance:** Controls the randomness of the fiber pattern.
  - **Strength:** Adjusts the contrast and definition of the fibers.
- **Lens Flare: (Filter > Render > Lens Flare)**
  - Simulates the effect of a bright light shining into the camera lens, creating lens flares and reflections.
  - **Brightness:** Controls the intensity of the flare.
  - **Flare Center:** Sets the location of the flare's center.
  - **Lens Type:** Choose from different lens types (50-300mm Zoom, 35mm Prime, 105mm Prime, or Movie Prime) to change the appearance of the flare.
- **Lighting Effects: (Filter > Render > Lighting Effects)**
  - Adds one or more light sources to an image, allowing you to create dramatic lighting effects.
  - **Presets:** Offers a variety of pre-configured lighting setups.
  - **Light Types:**
    - **Point:** Like a bare lightbulb, casting light in all directions.
    - **Spot:** Like a spotlight, casting a focused beam of light.
    - **Infinite:** Like a distant light source (e.g., the sun), casting parallel rays of light.
  - **Properties:** Adjust the color, intensity, and other properties of each light source.
  - **Texture Channel:** Allows you to use a grayscale channel as a texture map to create embossed or 3D lighting effects.

Tips for Using Render Filters:
- **Create new layers for Render filters** so you can adjust their blending mode, opacity, and other properties without affecting the underlying image.
- **Use layer masks** to selectively apply the effects.
- **Experiment with different settings** to achieve the desired look.

- **Combine Render filters with other filters and adjustments** to create more complex effects.

Neural Filters are a relatively new and exciting addition to Photoshop. They leverage the power of artificial intelligence (specifically, machine learning models) to perform complex image transformations that would be difficult or time-consuming to achieve with traditional tools.

Accessing Neural Filters:

- Go to **Filter > Neural Filters**.
- **Neural Filters Workspace:**
- **Featured Filters:** This section displays the currently available and fully released Neural Filters.
- **Beta Filters:** This section showcases filters that are still under development but can be tested. These may have limitations or produce unexpected results.
- **Wait List:** This section allows you to vote for filters you would like to see added to Photoshop in the future.
- **Filter List:** The right side of the workspace lists all available filters, including Featured and Beta.
- **Output:** Choose how you want to output the results of the filter:
  - **Current Layer:** Applies the filter directly to the current layer (destructive).
  - **Duplicate Layer:** Creates a new layer with the filter applied.
  - **Duplicate Layer Masked:** Creates a new layer with a mask that isolates the filter's effect.
  - **Smart Filter:** Applies the filter as a Smart Filter to a Smart Object (non-destructive).
  - **New Layer:** Creates a new layer containing only the pixels generated by the filter.

Important Considerations:
- **Internet Connection:** Many Neural Filters require an internet connection because they perform processing on Adobe's servers.
- **Performance:** Neural Filters can be computationally intensive, especially on older hardware.
- **Beta Filters:** Be aware that Beta filters are still under development and may not always produce perfect results.

Available Neural Filters:

Photoshop's Neural Filters are constantly evolving, with new filters and improvements being added regularly. As of the time of this writing, some of the available Neural Filters include:
- **Skin Smoothing:** Smooths skin in portraits while preserving details like hair and eyes.
- **Style Transfer:** Applies the artistic style of a selected image to your photo.
- **Smart Portrait:** Allows for significant alterations to a subject's facial features, including adjusting their expression, gaze, age, and hair.
- **JPEG Artifacts Removal:** Reduces artifacts caused by JPEG compression.

- **Super Zoom:** Allows for extreme enlargements of images, using AI to attempt to retain detail.
- **Depth-Aware Haze:** Adds atmospheric haze to an image, taking into account the perceived depth of objects in the scene.
- **Colorize:** Automatically colorizes black and white images.
- **Landscape Mixer:** Allows you to alter the appearance of a landscape, such as by changing the season or time of day.
- **Harmonization:** This filter attempts to harmonize the colors and tones of a composite image, making it look more realistic.
- **Makeup Transfer:** This filter transfers the makeup from one portrait to another.

Let's explore two of the popular Neural Filters in more detail:

10.9.1 Skin Smoothing

The Skin Smoothing filter is a powerful tool for retouching portraits. It uses AI to smooth skin while preserving important details like pores and hair.

How to Use Skin Smoothing:
1. Go to **Filter > Neural Filters**.
2. Enable the **Skin Smoothing** filter.
3. Adjust the **Blur** and **Smoothness** sliders to fine-tune the effect:
   - **Blur:** Controls the overall amount of blurring applied to the skin.
   - **Smoothness:** Adjusts the smoothness of the skin texture.
4. Choose an output option (e.g., Smart Filter for non-destructive editing).
5. Click **OK**.

Tips for Skin Smoothing:
- **Use a moderate amount of blur** to avoid making the skin look too artificial.
- **Zoom in to 100%** to accurately assess the effect.
- **Use a Smart Filter mask** to selectively apply the smoothing to specific areas of the face.
- **Combine Skin Smoothing with other retouching techniques** for more refined results.

10.9.2 Style Transfer

The Style Transfer filter allows you to apply the artistic style of a preset image or a custom image to your photo. It uses AI to analyze the style of the source image (e.g., brushstrokes, color palette, texture) and transfer those characteristics to your photo.

How to Use Style Transfer:
1. Go to **Filter > Neural Filters**.
2. Enable the **Style Transfer** filter.
3. Choose a preset style or click **Custom** and select an image to use as the style source.
4. Adjust the settings to fine-tune the effect:
   - **Style Transfer:** Check this box to apply the style transfer.
   - **Preserve Color:** Check this box to maintain the original colors of the image.
   - **Strength:** Controls the intensity of the style transfer.
   - **Style Detail:** Adjusts the level of detail from the style image that is applied.
   - **Brush Size:** Adjusts the size of the brush strokes if the selected style uses them.
   - **Focus on Subject:** Check this box to have Photoshop attempt to automatically detect and preserve the details of the main subject in the image.
   - **Brightness, Saturation, Preserve Details:** These settings allow for further fine-tuning of the result.
5. Choose an output option.
6. Click **OK**.

Tips for Style Transfer:
- **Experiment with different preset styles** to see which ones work best with your image.
- **Use a high-quality image** as your custom style source for the best results.
- **Adjust the Strength and Detail sliders** to fine-tune the effect.
- **Combine Style Transfer with other filters and adjustments** to create unique artistic looks.

10.9.3 Smart Portrait
The Smart Portrait filter is a powerful and somewhat controversial tool that allows you to make significant changes to a portrait subject's facial features, expression, age, gaze, and even hair thickness.

How to Use Smart Portrait:
1. Go to **Filter > Neural Filters**.
2. Enable the **Smart Portrait** filter. If using it for the first time, you may have to download it first.
3. Adjust the sliders to modify the portrait:
    - **Facial expressions:**
        1. **Happiness:** Makes the subject appear happier or more serious.
        2. **Surprise:** Adds a look of surprise.
        3. **Anger:** Adds a look of anger.
    - **Subject:**
        1. **Gaze:** Shifts the direction of the subject's eyes.
        2. **Head Direction:** Turns the subject's head.
        3. **Age:** Makes the subject appear older or younger.
        4. **Hair Thickness:** Increases or decreases the apparent thickness of the subject's hair.
        5. **Light Direction:** Changes the direction of the lighting on the subject.
4. Choose an output option (e.g., Smart Filter for non-destructive editing).
5. Click **OK**.

Tips for Smart Portrait:
- **Use subtle adjustments for realistic results.** Extreme changes can look artificial and uncanny.
- **Pay attention to the lighting.** The Light Direction slider can help to match the lighting after adjusting the head's position.
- **Be mindful of the ethical implications** of significantly altering a person's appearance.

10.9.4 Makeup Transfer
The Makeup Transfer filter allows you to transfer the makeup style from one image to another.

How to Use Makeup Transfer:

1. Go to **Filter > Neural Filters**.
2. Enable the **Makeup Transfer** filter.
3. **Reference Image:** Select a reference image from the dropdown, or select Custom to upload your own. This image should contain the makeup look you want to transfer.
4. Choose an output option.
5. Click **OK**.

Tips for Makeup Transfer:

- **Use high-quality source images** for the best results.
- **The source and target images should have similar face shapes and angles** for optimal transfer.

10.9.5 Depth-Aware Haze

Depth-Aware Haze adds atmospheric haze to an image, taking into account the perceived depth of objects in the scene. This can be used to create a sense of distance or to add a stylistic effect.

How to Use Depth-Aware Haze:

1. Go to **Filter > Neural Filters**.
2. Enable the **Depth-Aware Haze** filter.
3. Adjust the sliders to fine-tune the effect:
   - **Haze:** Controls the amount of haze.
   - **Warmth:** Adjusts the color temperature of the haze.
   - **Depth:** Adjust the depth range slider to change the perceived distance of objects that are affected by the haze.

Tips for Depth-Aware Haze:

- **Use a landscape image with a clear sense of depth** for the best results.
- **Experiment with different Warmth settings** to create different moods.

10.9.6 Colorize

The Colorize filter uses AI to automatically colorize black and white images.

How to Use Colorize:

1. Go to **Filter > Neural Filters**.
2. Enable the **Colorize** filter.
3. Adjust the **Profile**, **Strength**, and **Color Balance** sliders.
4. Manually adjust colors by selecting an area within the preview and choosing a new color.
5. Choose an output option.
6. Click **OK**.

Tips for Colorize:

- **The AI does a surprisingly good job in many cases,** but you may need to make manual adjustments for optimal results.
- **Use the filter on a duplicate layer or as a Smart Filter** so you can go back and refine the colors.

10.9.7 Super Zoom

Super Zoom allows you to zoom in and crop a portion of an image, and it uses AI to enhance the detail and resolution of the cropped area.

How to Use Super Zoom:
1. Go to **Filter > Neural Filters**.
2. Enable the **Super Zoom** filter.
3. **Use the zoom and pan controls** in the preview window to select the area you want to crop.

4. Adjust the sliders to fine-tune the enhancement:

   - **Reduce Noise:** Reduces noise in the zoomed image.
   - **Sharpen:** Sharpens details.
   - **Enhance Face:** Improves the detail and clarity of faces.
   - **Remove JPEG Artifacts:** Reduces compression artifacts.

5. Choose an output option.
6. Click **OK**.

Tips for Super Zoom:

- **Don't expect miracles.** While Super Zoom can enhance details, it can't create information that wasn't there in the original image.
- **Use it judiciously.** Extreme zooms may still produce noticeable artifacts.

10.9.8 JPEG Artifacts Removal

The JPEG Artifacts Removal filter attempts to reduce the blockiness and other artifacts that can result from JPEG compression.

How to Use JPEG Artifacts Removal:
1. Go to **Filter > Neural Filters**.
2. Enable the **JPEG Artifacts Removal** filter.
3. Choose an output option.
4. Click **OK**.

Tips for JPEG Artifacts Removal:
- **This filter works best on images with mild to moderate JPEG artifacts.**

10.9.9 Landscape Mixer

The Landscape Mixer filter is a creative tool that allows you to alter the appearance of a landscape image by blending it with the characteristics of another landscape image, such as changing the season or time of day.

How to Use Landscape Mixer:
1. Go to **Filter > Neural Filters**.
2. Enable the **Landscape Mixer** filter.
3. Select a preset or upload your own custom landscape image in the **Custom** section.
4. Adjust the sliders to fine-tune the effect. These may include sliders for the season, time of day, and overall strength of the effect.
5. Choose an output option.
6. Click **OK**.

Tips for Landscape Mixer:
- **Experiment with different presets and custom images** to see the wide range of possibilities.
- **Use the Strength slider to control the intensity of the transformation.**

10.9.10 Harmonization

The Harmonization filter is designed to make composite images more believable by harmonizing the color and tone of one layer with another. This is especially useful when combining elements from different sources that have different lighting or color characteristics.

How to use Harmonization:
1. Select the layer you want to adjust. This is often a foreground element that you have composited onto a background.
2. Go to **Filter > Neural Filters**.
3. Enable the **Harmonization** filter.

4. In the **Reference Image** section, choose the layer you want to harmonize with (usually the background layer).

5. Adjust the sliders to fine-tune the effect:
   - **Strength:** Controls the overall intensity of the harmonization.
   - **Brightness:** Adjusts the brightness of the selected layer to match the reference layer.
   - **Saturation:** Adjusts the color saturation of the selected layer.
   - **Cyan-Red, Magenta-Green, Yellow-Blue:** These sliders allow for fine adjustments to the color balance.

6. Choose an output option.

7. Click **OK**.

Tips for Harmonization:
- **Use this filter on Smart Objects** so you can readjust the settings later.
- **Pay attention to the edges of the composited element** to make sure they blend seamlessly with the background.

10.9.11 Other Neural Filters

- **Wait List:** The "Wait List" section of the Neural Filters panel allows you to see and vote for filters that are being considered for development. Some filters might move from "Wait List" to "Beta," and eventually to "Featured."

Keep in mind that the available Neural Filters and their functionality are constantly evolving. Be sure to check the Neural Filters panel regularly for updates and new additions.

10.10 Working with Third-Party Filters

In addition to Photoshop's built-in filters and Neural Filters, you can also install and use third-party filters (also known as plugins) to extend Photoshop's capabilities. These filters are developed by other companies and individuals and offer a vast range of effects and tools.

Where to Find Third-Party Filters:
- **Adobe Exchange:** A marketplace for extensions, including filters, for Creative Cloud apps.
- **Developer Websites:** Many software developers offer Photoshop filters directly from their websites.

Installing Third-Party Filters:

- The installation process varies depending on the filter. Some filters come with their own installers, while others need to be manually copied into Photoshop's Plug-Ins folder.
- **Refer to the installation instructions provided by the filter developer.**

Accessing Third-Party Filters:
- Once installed, third-party filters usually appear under the **Filter** menu, often in their own submenu.
- Some third-party filters may have their own separate panels or interfaces.

Popular Third-Party Filter Developers:
- **Topaz Labs:** Offers a suite of filters for noise reduction, sharpening, image enlargement, and more.
- **Nik Collection by DxO:** A popular collection of filters for various tasks, including color correction, black and white conversion, and HDR effects.
- **ON1:** Develops a range of filters and plugins for photo editing and effects.
- **Exposure Software:** Offers filters that simulate the look of analog film and other creative effects.
- **Alien Skin:** (Now part of Exposure Software) Known for creative filters and effects.

10.11 Using Generative AI to Create Custom Filters

This is a more speculative area, but as AI technology continues to advance, it's becoming increasingly possible to use generative AI to create custom filters or effects. This could involve:

- **Training AI models on specific datasets of images** to learn particular styles or transformations.
- **Using text prompts or other inputs** to guide the AI in generating new filters.
- **Developing AI-powered tools** that allow users to create their own filters by adjusting parameters or providing examples.

Potential Applications:

- **Creating unique artistic styles:** Imagine being able to train an AI on the work of your favorite painter and then apply that style to your photos in Photoshop.
- **Automating complex editing tasks:** You could potentially create custom filters that perform a series of adjustments and transformations with a single click.
- **Developing new visual effects:** AI could be used to generate entirely new types of filters and effects that were previously unimaginable.

Challenges:

- **Technical Complexity:** Developing these tools requires significant expertise in AI and machine learning.
- **Computational Resources:** Training and running complex AI models can be computationally expensive.
- **User Interface:** Designing user-friendly interfaces for creating and using AI-generated filters will be a challenge.

While still in its early stages, the use of generative AI for creating custom filters holds immense potential for the future of image editing. It's an area that's likely to see significant development in the coming years.

Transforming and Manipulating Images

Photoshop offers a wide range of tools for transforming and manipulating images, allowing you to resize, reshape, rotate, distort, and adjust the perspective of your photos. These tools are essential for compositing, correcting distortions, and achieving creative effects. This chapter will explore the most important transformation tools and techniques, from basic cropping and resizing to advanced warping and perspective adjustments.

11.1 Cropping and Straightening Images

Cropping is the process of removing unwanted portions of an image to improve its composition, change its aspect ratio, or focus attention on a specific subject. Straightening is used to correct images that were taken with a tilted camera.

The Crop Tool:
- **Select the Crop Tool (C)** from the Tools Panel.
- **Crop Overlay:** A cropping overlay will appear on your image, with handles on the corners and sides.
- **Adjusting the Crop:**
  - **Drag the handles** to resize the crop area.
  - **Click and drag inside the crop area** to reposition it.
  - **Click and drag outside the crop area** to rotate it. This can be used to straighten an image.
- **Aspect Ratio:** In the Options Bar, you can choose a specific aspect ratio from the drop-down menu (e.g., 1:1 for a square, 4:3, 16:9) or enter custom dimensions.
- **Straighten Tool:** Click the **Straighten** icon in the Options Bar, then draw a line along an edge in your image that should be horizontal or vertical. Photoshop will automatically rotate the image to straighten it. You can choose for Photoshop to automatically crop out the rotated edges or fill them in using Content-Aware technology.
- **Delete Cropped Pixels:**
  - **Checked:** Permanently deletes the pixels outside the crop area.
  - **Unchecked:** Hides the pixels outside the crop area, allowing you to readjust the crop later. This is the non-destructive option and is generally recommended.
- **Content-Aware:** When this option is checked, Photoshop will attempt to fill in any blank areas created by the crop using Content-Aware technology.
- **Overlay Options:** You can choose different overlay options to help with composition, such as the Rule of Thirds, Grid, or Golden Ratio.
- **Commit the Crop:** Press **Enter/Return** or click the checkmark in the Options Bar to apply the crop.

Tips for Cropping:

- **Consider the composition.** Use the crop tool to improve the overall balance and visual appeal of your image.
- **Use the Rule of Thirds** or other compositional guidelines to help you place your subject effectively.
- **Maintain a suitable aspect ratio** for your intended output (e.g., 4:3 for standard prints, 16:9 for widescreen displays).

11.2 Resizing Images: Image Size vs. Canvas Size

Resizing images is a common task in Photoshop. It's important to understand the difference between **Image Size** and **Canvas Size**:
- **Image Size:** Changes the dimensions and/or resolution of the image itself, affecting the number of pixels in the image.
- **Canvas Size:** Changes the size of the "canvas" on which the image sits, adding or removing space around the image without affecting the image data itself.

Image Size:
- Go to **Image > Image Size**.
- **Resample:**
  - **Checked:** Allows you to change the number of pixels in the image (resampling). This is necessary if you want to change the print dimensions without affecting the resolution, or if you want to significantly enlarge the image.
    - **Resampling Methods:** Choose an appropriate resampling method based on the type of image and whether you're enlarging or reducing it:
      - **Automatic:** Photoshop chooses the best method.
      - **Preserve Details (enlargement):** Good for enlarging images while preserving details.
      - **Bicubic Smoother (enlargement):** Good for smooth enlargements.
      - **Bicubic Sharper (reduction):** Good for reducing image size while preserving sharpness.
      - **Bicubic (smooth gradients):** A good all-around method for resampling.
      - **Nearest Neighbor (hard edges):** Preserves hard edges but can result in a pixelated look. Use for pixel art.
      - **Bilinear:** Averages the colors of surrounding pixels; faster but less precise than Bicubic.
  - **Unchecked:** Links the width, height, and resolution, allowing you to change the print dimensions without changing the number of pixels.
- **Width and Height:** Enter the desired dimensions in pixels, inches, centimeters, or other units.
- **Resolution:** Enter the desired resolution in pixels per inch (PPI). Remember that 300 PPI is generally recommended for high-quality printing, while 72 PPI is often used for web images.

- **Constrain Proportions:** Check this option to maintain the original aspect ratio of the image when resizing.

Canvas Size:

- Go to **Image > Canvas Size**.
- **Current Size:** Displays the current dimensions of the canvas.
- **New Size:** Enter the desired dimensions for the new canvas.
- **Anchor:** Click on the squares in the Anchor grid to specify the direction in which the canvas should be expanded or which part of the image should be kept when the canvas is reduced.
- **Relative:** Check this option to add or subtract a specific amount of space to the canvas, rather than entering absolute dimensions.
- **Canvas extension color:** Choose the color to use for the newly added canvas area.

Use Cases:

- **Image Size:** Use this when you need to change the actual dimensions or resolution of your image, for example, to prepare it for printing at a specific size or to reduce its file size for web use.
- **Canvas Size:** Use this when you need to add more space around your image, for example, to create a border or to add room for text or other elements. You can also use it to crop an image by reducing the canvas size.

11.3 Rotating and Flipping Images

Rotating and flipping are basic but essential transformations.

Rotating:

- **Image > Image Rotation:**
  - **180°:** Rotates the image 180 degrees.
  - **90° Clockwise:** Rotates the image 90 degrees to the right.
  - **90° Counter Clockwise:** Rotates the image 90 degrees to the left.
  - **Arbitrary:** Allows you to enter a specific rotation angle.
  - **Flip Canvas Horizontal:** Flips the image horizontally.
  - **Flip Canvas Vertical:** Flips the image vertically.

Flipping:

- **Edit > Transform > Flip Horizontal:** Flips the selected layer horizontally.
- **Edit > Transform > Flip Vertical:** Flips the selected layer vertically.

11.4 Free Transform: Scaling, Rotating, Skewing, Distorting, and Perspective

Free Transform is a versatile tool that allows you to perform a variety of transformations on a layer or selection, including scaling, rotating, skewing, distorting, and applying perspective.

How to Use Free Transform:

- **Select the layer or area** you want to transform.
- Go to **Edit > Free Transform** or use the keyboard shortcut **Ctrl+T (Windows)** or **Cmd+T (macOS)**.
- **Transform Handles:** A bounding box with handles will appear around the selected area.
- **Perform Transformations:**
    - **Scale:** Drag any of the corner handles to resize the image. Hold down **Shift** to maintain the aspect ratio while scaling. Hold down **Alt (Windows) / Option (macOS)** to scale from the center.
    - **Rotate:** Move your cursor outside the bounding box until it turns into a curved double arrow, then click and drag to rotate. Hold down **Shift** to constrain the rotation to 15-degree increments.
    - **Skew:** Hold down **Ctrl (Windows) / Cmd (macOS)** and drag a side handle to skew the image.
    - **Distort:** Hold down **Ctrl+Alt (Windows) / Cmd+Option (macOS)** and drag a corner handle to freely distort the image.
    - **Perspective:** Hold down **Ctrl+Alt+Shift (Windows) / Cmd+Option+Shift (macOS)** and drag a corner handle to apply perspective.
    - **Warp:** Click the **Switch between free transform and warp modes** button in the Options Bar to access a grid that allows for more complex warping.
    - **Move:** Click inside the bounding box and drag to reposition the image.
- **Commit the Transformation:** Press **Enter/Return** or click the checkmark in the Options Bar.

Options Bar:

- **Reference Point:** The small square icon in the Options Bar determines the point around which transformations are performed. You can click on different parts of the icon to change the reference point.
- **X and Y:** Specify the horizontal and vertical position of the reference point.
- **W and H:** Specify the width and height of the transformed object.

- **Maintain Aspect Ratio:** The chain icon between W and H allows you to link or unlink the width and height, maintaining the aspect ratio while scaling.
- **Rotation Angle:** Enter a specific rotation angle.
- **Skew:** Enter specific values for horizontal and vertical skew.
- **Warp:** Switch to warp mode.
- **Cancel/Commit:** Cancel or commit the transformation.

Tips for Free Transform:
- **Use Smart Objects** to perform transformations non-destructively.
- **Hold down modifier keys** to access different transformation modes.
- **Use the Reference Point** to control the center of rotation or scaling.

11.5 Warp Tool: Advanced Image Manipulation

The Warp tool provides a flexible way to distort and reshape images by manipulating a grid that overlays the selected area.

How to Use the Warp Tool:
1. **Select the layer or area** you want to warp.
2. Go to **Edit > Transform > Warp** or enter Free Transform (**Ctrl+T / Cmd+T**) and then click the **Switch between free transform and warp modes** button in the Options Bar.
3. **Warp Grid:** A grid will appear over the selected area.
4. **Manipulate the Grid:**
   - **Drag the grid points** to distort the image.
   - **Drag the Bezier handles** that appear when you click on a grid point to adjust the curvature of the warp.
   - **Click and drag inside the grid** to warp that specific area.
5. **Options Bar:**
   - **Warp:** Choose from a variety of preset warp styles (e.g., Arch, Bulge, Flag, Fish).
   - **Bend:** Controls the intensity of the warp.
   - **Horizontal/Vertical Distortion:** Applies additional horizontal or vertical distortion.
6. **Commit the Warp:** Press **Enter/Return** or click the checkmark in the Options Bar.

Tips for Using the Warp Tool:
- **Use Smart Objects** for non-destructive warping.
- **Add more grid points** for finer control by clicking on the grid lines.
- **Experiment with different preset warp styles** to get a feel for the possibilities.
- **Use the Warp tool in conjunction with other transformation tools** for even more complex manipulations.

11.6 Puppet Warp: Precise Control over Image Elements

Puppet Warp is a powerful tool that allows you to reposition and deform parts of an image by placing and manipulating pins, as if you were controlling a puppet. It's particularly useful for adjusting the pose of a figure, repositioning limbs, or correcting distortions.

How to Use Puppet Warp:
1. **Select the layer** you want to warp.
2. Go to **Edit > Puppet Warp**.
3. **Add Pins:** Click on the image to add pins to the areas you want to control. Think of these as joints or points of articulation.
4. **Manipulate Pins:**
   - **Drag pins** to reposition them, deforming the image.
   - **Select multiple pins** by holding down **Shift** and clicking on them.
   - **Rotate pins:** Hover your cursor near a pin until it turns into a curved double arrow, then click and drag to rotate.
   - **Remove pins:** Select a pin and press **Delete**, or **Alt-click (Windows) / Option-click (macOS)** on a pin.
5. **Options Bar:**
   - **Mode:**
     1. **Normal:** Provides a good balance between rigidity and elasticity.
     2. **Rigid:** Makes the image more resistant to deformation.
     3. **Distort:** Allows for more extreme deformations.
   - **Density:** Controls the number of mesh points generated. More points provide greater control but can be more computationally intensive.
   - **Expansion:** Expands or contracts the mesh beyond the edges of the object.
   - **Show Mesh:** Toggles the visibility of the mesh.
   - **Pin Depth:** Use the up and down arrow icons to move pins in front of or behind other pins. This can help to resolve overlapping issues.
   - **Rotate:** Choose between Auto and Fixed to control how pins rotate.
6. **Commit the Warp:** Press **Enter/Return** or click the checkmark in the Options Bar.

Tips for Using Puppet Warp:
- **Use Smart Objects** for non-destructive editing.
- **Place pins strategically** along joints, edges, and areas that need to be controlled.
- **Use the Pin Depth** buttons to manage overlapping areas.

11.7 Content-Aware Scale: Intelligently Resizing Images

Content-Aware Scale is a remarkable tool that allows you to resize an image while preserving important content and minimizing distortion. It intelligently analyzes the image and attempts to protect areas with significant details (like people or objects) while scaling areas with less important content (like backgrounds).

How to Use Content-Aware Scale:
1. **Select the layer** you want to resize.
2. Go to **Edit > Content-Aware Scale**.
3. **Scaling Handles:** Scaling handles will appear around the image, similar to Free Transform.

4. **Scale the Image:** Drag the handles to resize the image. Photoshop will attempt to preserve the proportions of important content while scaling the rest.
5. **Options Bar:**
   o **Protect:** Choose an alpha channel from the drop-down menu to protect specific areas from scaling. You can create an alpha channel by saving a selection (see Chapter 5).
   o **Amount:** Specifies the ratio between normal scaling and content-aware scaling. At 100%, all scaling is content-aware. At 0%, all scaling is normal.
   o **Reference Point:** Specifies the fixed point from which the image is scaled.
6. **Commit the Scaling:** Press **Enter/Return** or click the checkmark in the Options Bar.

Tips for Using Content-Aware Scale:

- **Create an alpha channel to protect important areas** from scaling.
- **Use Content-Aware Scale in conjunction with other transformation tools** for more complex resizing tasks.
- **Content-Aware Scale works best on images with clearly defined subjects and backgrounds.**

Perspective Warp is an advanced tool for correcting or manipulating the perspective in an image. It's particularly useful for architectural photography, where you might need to straighten converging lines or adjust the perspective to make a building appear more imposing.

How to Use Perspective Warp:

1. **Select the layer** you want to adjust.
2. Go to **Edit > Perspective Warp**.
3. **Define the Planes (Layout Mode):**
   - The initial mode is **Layout**. In this mode, you define the planes of the perspective you want to adjust.
   - **Draw quadrilaterals** along the planes of your image. For example, for a building, you might draw quads along the walls and the ground. The quads should be aligned with the perspective lines of the image.
4. **Warp the Planes (Warp Mode):**
   - Click the **Warp** button in the Options Bar to switch to Warp mode.
   - **Drag the pins** at the corners of the quads to adjust the perspective.
   - **Shift-click** on a line to make it vertical or horizontal.
   - **Click the auto-straighten buttons** in the Options bar (Vertical, Horizontal, or both) to automatically straighten lines based on your defined quads.
5. **Commit the Warp:** Press **Enter/Return** or click the checkmark in the Options Bar.

Tips for Using Perspective Warp:

- **Use Smart Objects** for non-destructive editing.
- **Define the planes carefully in Layout mode.** The accuracy of your quads will determine the quality of the perspective adjustment.
- **Use the auto-straighten buttons** as a starting point, but be prepared to make manual adjustments as well.

Working with Type

Typography is a powerful design element that can add impact and clarity to your images. Photoshop offers a robust set of tools for working with type, allowing you to add text, control its formatting, create text on a path, warp and distort text, and even work with 3D text. This chapter will explore the essential type tools and techniques in Photoshop.

12.1 The Type Tool: Adding Text to Your Images

The Type Tool is the primary tool for adding text to your Photoshop documents.

Types of Type Tools:
- **Horizontal Type Tool (T):** Creates horizontal text. This is the most common type tool.
- **Vertical Type Tool (T):** Creates vertical text.
- **Horizontal Type Mask Tool (T):** Creates a selection in the shape of horizontal text.
- **Vertical Type Mask Tool (T):** Creates a selection in the shape of vertical text.

Adding Point Type:
1. **Select the Horizontal Type Tool (T)** from the Tools Panel.
2. **Click** in your document where you want to add text. A blinking cursor will appear, indicating the text insertion point.
3. **Start typing.**
4. **Commit the text:** Press **Enter** on the numeric keypad, click the checkmark in the Options Bar, or **Ctrl+Enter (Windows) / Cmd+Return (macOS)**.

Adding Paragraph Type:
1. **Select the Horizontal Type Tool (T)**.
2. **Click and drag** in your document to create a text box.
3. **Start typing.** The text will automatically wrap within the boundaries of the text box.
4. **Commit the text:** Press **Enter** on the numeric keypad, click the checkmark in the Options Bar, or **Ctrl+Enter (Windows) / Cmd+Return (macOS)**.

Options Bar:
When the Type Tool is active, the Options Bar displays various settings for formatting text:
- **Font Family:** Choose a font from the drop-down menu.
- **Font Style:** Select a style for the font (e.g., Regular, Bold, Italic).
- **Font Size:** Set the size of the text in points (pt).
- **Anti-aliasing:** Controls the smoothness of the text edges. Options include: None, Sharp, Crisp, Strong, and Smooth.
- **Alignment:** Align the text to the left, center, or right.
- **Text Color:** Set the color of the text.
- **Warp Text:** Apply warping effects to the text.
- **Character/Paragraph Panels:** Open the Character and Paragraph panels for more advanced text options.
- **3D Mode:** Switches to 3D mode for working with 3D text.

12.2 Formatting Text: Font, Size, Color, Alignment, and More

Once you've added text to your document, you can format it using the Options Bar, the Character panel, or the Paragraph panel.

Basic Formatting:

1. **Font Family:** Choose a font that suits the style and purpose of your design.
2. **Font Style:** Select a font style to add emphasis or visual interest.
3. **Font Size:** Adjust the size of the text to make it readable and visually balanced.
4. **Text Color:** Choose a color that contrasts well with the background and complements the overall design.
5. **Alignment:**
   - **Left Alignment:** Aligns the text to the left edge of the text box or point type.
   - **Center Alignment:** Centers the text within the text box or on the point type's insertion point.
   - **Right Alignment:** Aligns the text to the right edge of the text box or point type.
6. **Justification:** (Paragraph type only) Controls how the text is distributed between the left and right edges of the text box. Options include: Left Justify, Center Justify, Right Justify, and Full Justify (which justifies all lines except the last).
7. **Anti-aliasing:** Choose an anti-aliasing method to smooth the edges of the text. Sharp generally produces the crispest results.

12.3 Character and Paragraph Panels: Advanced Text Options

The Character and Paragraph panels provide a wide range of advanced options for fine-tuning the appearance of your text.

Accessing the Panels:

- Go to **Window > Character** or **Window > Paragraph**.
- Click the **Character/Paragraph Panels** button in the Options Bar when the Type Tool is active.

Character Panel:

- **Font Family, Style, Size, Color:** Same as in the Options Bar.
- **Leading:** Controls the vertical space between lines of text.
- **Kerning:** Adjusts the space between two specific characters.
- **Tracking:** Adjusts the space between a range of characters.
- **Vertical Scale:** Stretches the text vertically.
- **Horizontal Scale:** Stretches the text horizontally.
- **Baseline Shift:** Moves selected characters above or below the baseline.
- **Faux Bold, Faux Italic:** Applies simulated bold or italic styling to fonts that don't have those styles available.

- **All Caps, Small Caps, Superscript, Subscript, Underline, Strikethrough:** Various character formatting options.
- **Language:** Specifies the language for hyphenation and spell-checking.
- **Paragraph Panel:**
- **Alignment and Justification:** Same as in the Options Bar.
- **Indentation:** Indent the left or right edges of the paragraph, or indent only the first line.
- **Space Before/After:** Adds space before or after paragraphs.
- **Hyphenation:** Turns hyphenation on or off and allows you to customize hyphenation settings.

Tips for Formatting Text:
- **Choose fonts carefully.** Select fonts that are appropriate for the tone and purpose of your design.
- **Use a limited number of fonts.** Too many different fonts can make a design look cluttered and unprofessional.
- **Pay attention to leading, kerning, and tracking** to ensure that your text is readable and visually appealing.
- **Use paragraph styles** to create and apply consistent formatting to multiple text elements.

12.4 Creating and Editing Text on a Path

Photoshop allows you to create text that follows a curved or irregular path, adding a dynamic element to your designs.

Creating Text on a Path:
1. **Create a path:** Use the **Pen tool** or any of the **shape tools** to create a path.
2. **Select the Horizontal Type Tool (T).**
3. **Move your cursor over the path.** The cursor will change to an I-beam with a curved line through it.
4. **Click on the path** where you want the text to begin.
5. **Start typing.** The text will follow the path.

Editing Text on a Path:

- **Select the text layer** in the Layers Panel.
- **Use the Direct Selection Tool (A)** to adjust the path. The text will reflow along the modified path.
- **Use the Path Selection Tool (A)** to move the entire path, including the text.
- **Use the Type Tool** to edit the text itself, change its formatting, or adjust its position on the path. You can control where the text starts and ends on the path using the start and end point brackets.

Options for Text on a Path:

- When you select text on a path with either selection tool, an X will appear on the path where you originally clicked. This is the start point.

- If you hover to the left or right of the start point, you will see a cursor with a left or right arrow. You can use this cursor to drag the text along the path.

- If you drag the start point, this will move the text along the path.

- There will also be an end point marker that can be similarly adjusted.

- When selecting text on a path with the **Type Tool**, the Options Bar will show additional options:
  - **Path Options:** This button opens the Path Options dialog, where you can further customize how the text flows along the path.
    - **Flip:** Flips the text to the other side of the path.
    - **3D Ribbon, Stair Step, Gravity:** These options affect how the characters are oriented in relation to the path.
    - **Align to Path:** Choose how the text aligns to the path: Baseline, Ascender, Descender, or Center.
    - **Spacing:** Adjusts the spacing between characters along the path.

12.5 Warping Text for Creative Effects

The Warp Text feature allows you to distort text in a variety of ways, creating interesting visual effects.

How to Warp Text:

1. **Select the text layer** you want to warp.
2. **Click the Warp Text button** in the Options Bar (it looks like a curved grid with a T above it).

Warp Text Dialog Box:

- **Style:** Choose a preset warp style from the drop-down menu (e.g., Arc, Bulge, Flag, Fish).
- **Bend:** Controls the intensity of the warp.
- **Horizontal/Vertical Distortion:** Applies additional horizontal or vertical distortion.
- **Orientation:** Switch between a horizontal or vertical warp.

Tips for Warping Text:

- **Use warping sparingly.** Too much distortion can make text difficult to read.
- **Experiment with different warp styles** to see which ones work best for your design.
- **You can edit the text after it's been warped**, but the changes will be constrained by the existing warp.
- **Convert the text layer to a Smart Object** before warping to preserve the ability to edit the text and the warp settings later.

12.6 Using Type as a Mask

You can use the **Horizontal Type Mask Tool** or the **Vertical Type Mask Tool** to create selections in the shape of text. This allows you to use text as a mask, revealing or hiding parts of an underlying layer.

How to Use the Type Mask Tools:
1. **Select the Horizontal Type Mask Tool or Vertical Type Mask Tool** from the Tools Panel.
2. **Click in your document** or **click and drag** to create a text box.
3. **Type your text.** The text will appear as a red overlay (similar to Quick Mask mode).
4. **Commit the text:** Press **Enter** on the numeric keypad, click the checkmark in the Options Bar, or **Ctrl+Enter (Windows) / Cmd+Return (macOS)**.
5. **A selection** in the shape of the text will appear.

Using the Text Selection as a Mask:
- **Create a layer mask:** With the selection active, click the **Add layer mask** button at the bottom of the Layers Panel.
- **Fill the selection:** Use the **Paint Bucket Tool** or the **Edit > Fill** command to fill the selection with a color or pattern.
- **Apply adjustments:** With the selection active, apply adjustment layers to affect only the area within the text selection.

12.7 Working with 3D Text

Photoshop allows you to create and manipulate 3D text, adding depth and dimension to your designs.

Note: 3D features are being gradually phased out of Photoshop. While they might still be available in Photoshop 2025, their functionality might be limited, and they may be removed in future versions. This section is provided for legacy purposes.

Creating 3D Text:
1. **Select a type layer.**
2. Go to **3D > New 3D Extrusion from Selected Layer**.

3D Workspace:
- Photoshop will switch to the 3D workspace, which contains specialized tools and panels for working with 3D objects.
- **3D Panel:** Lists all the components of your 3D scene, including meshes, materials, and lights.
- **Properties Panel:** Provides settings for the selected 3D object, such as extrusion depth, bevel, and inflation.
- **Move Tool (3D Mode):** When in 3D mode, the Move Tool has additional controls for rotating, scaling, and repositioning 3D objects.

Manipulating 3D Text:
- **Extrusion Depth:** Controls how far the text is extruded in 3D space.

- **Bevel:** Adds a beveled edge to the text.
- **Inflation:** Creates a rounded, inflated look.
- **Materials:** Apply different materials and textures to the 3D text.
- **Lighting:** Adjust the lighting of the 3D scene to enhance the 3D effect.
- **Camera Position:** Change the camera angle to view the 3D text from different perspectives.

Rendering 3D Text:

- When you're finished editing your 3D text, you'll need to render the scene to create the final, high-quality 3D effect. The rendering process can take some time, depending on the complexity of the scene and your computer's processing power.
- You can render the scene by going to **3D > Render 3D Layer**.

This concludes Chapter 12! You've now explored the essential tools and techniques for working with type in Photoshop. You've learned how to add and format text, create text on a path, warp text, use type as a mask, and even delve into the world of 3D text. With these skills, you can add impactful typography to your designs and create visually engaging text effects.

Painting and Brushes

Photoshop offers a powerful and versatile painting engine, allowing you to create digital artwork, retouch photos, and add painterly effects to your designs. The heart of this painting system is the Brush Tool, which, along with its many customizable settings and related tools like the Mixer Brush and Pencil, provides a wide range of creative possibilities. This chapter will explore the essentials of painting in Photoshop, from basic brushwork to advanced brush dynamics and simulating real-world painting techniques.

13.1 The Brush Tool: An Overview

The Brush Tool (B) is one of the most fundamental tools in Photoshop. It allows you to paint with the foreground color using a variety of brush tips and settings.

Selecting the Brush Tool:
- Click the **Brush Tool (B)** icon in the Tools Panel.

Basic Brush Usage:
1. **Choose a Brush Preset:** Select a brush tip from the Brush Preset picker in the Options Bar or the Brush Settings panel.
2. **Set the Foreground Color:** Click the Foreground Color swatch in the Tools Panel to open the Color Picker and choose your desired color.
3. **Adjust Brush Size:**
   - Use the **[** and **]** keys to decrease or increase the brush size.
   - Right-click (Windows) or Control-click (macOS) in the document window to open the Brush Preset picker and adjust the **Size** slider.
4. **Adjust Brush Hardness:**
   - Hold down **Shift** and use the **[** and **]** keys to decrease or increase the brush hardness.
   - Right-click (Windows) or Control-click (macOS) in the document window to open the Brush Preset picker and adjust the **Hardness** slider. A hardness of 100% creates a hard-edged brush stroke, while 0% creates a soft, feathered stroke.
5. **Paint in your document:** Click and drag to paint.

Options Bar:
When the Brush Tool is active, the Options Bar displays various settings for controlling the brush:
- **Brush Preset Picker:** Allows you to choose from a variety of preset brush tips.
- **Mode:** Sets the blending mode for the brush. Normal is the default, but you can choose from other modes like Multiply, Screen, Overlay, etc.
- **Opacity:** Controls the transparency of the brush strokes.
- **Flow:** Determines the rate at which paint is applied. A lower flow allows you to build up color gradually with multiple strokes.

- **Smoothing:** This setting helps to smooth out your brush strokes, making them appear less jagged.
- **Angle:** Sets the angle of the brush tip.
- **Use Pressure for Opacity:** (Pen Pressure icon) When using a pressure-sensitive tablet, this option controls opacity with pen pressure.
- **Use Pressure for Size:** (Airbrush icon) When using a pressure-sensitive tablet, this option controls size with pen pressure.
- **Always Use Pressure for Size:** When this is enabled, your brush size will be controlled by your tablet's pressure sensitivity.
- **Symmetry Options:** This allows you to paint with various types of symmetry, such as vertical, horizontal, or radial.

13.2 Brush Presets and Customizing Brushes

Photoshop comes with a wide range of preset brushes, and you can also create and customize your own.

Brush Preset Picker:
- **Accessing the Brush Preset Picker:**
  - Click the Brush Preset Picker icon in the Options Bar.
  - Right-click (Windows) or Control-click (macOS) in the document window while the Brush Tool is active.
- **Choosing a Brush:** Click on a brush thumbnail to select it.
- **Brush Categories:** The Brush Preset Picker is organized into categories (e.g., General Brushes, Dry Media Brushes, Wet Media Brushes, Special Effect Brushes).
- **Loading More Brushes:**
  - Click the gear icon in the upper-right corner of the Brush Preset Picker.
  - Choose **Import Brushes** to load brush sets (.abr files) that you've downloaded or created.
  - You can also choose from a list of additional brush sets that come with Photoshop.
- **Managing Presets:** The Preset Manager (**Edit > Presets > Preset Manager**) allows you to organize, rename, delete, and save brush presets.

Brush Settings Panel:
The Brush Settings panel (**Window > Brush Settings**) provides a comprehensive set of options for customizing brushes.
- **Brush Tip Shape:**
  - **Diameter:** Controls the size of the brush tip.
  - **Hardness:** Adjusts the softness of the brush edge.
  - **Spacing:** Determines the distance between individual brush marks in a stroke.
  - **Angle:** Rotates the brush tip.

- o **Roundness:** Changes the shape of the brush tip from round to elliptical.
- o **Flip X/Flip Y:** Flips the brush tip horizontally or vertically.
- **Shape Dynamics:** (Covered in the next section)
- **Scattering:** (Covered in the next section)
- **Texture:** (Covered in the next section)
- **Other Categories:** The Brush Settings panel has many other categories, including Dual Brush, Color Dynamics, Transfer, and more. These allow for a vast range of customization options.

Creating Custom Brushes:

1. **Define a Brush Preset:**

   - o Create the shape or image you want to use as a brush tip. It's often best to work in black and white when creating custom brushes.

   - o Go to **Edit > Define Brush Preset**.
   - o Give your brush a name and click **OK**.

2. **Customize the Brush:** Open the Brush Settings panel to adjust the brush's dynamics, texture, and other properties.

3. **Save the Brush:** You can save your customized brush as a new preset by clicking the **New Brush Preset** icon at the bottom of the Brush Settings panel or by choosing **New Brush Preset** from the Brush Preset Picker's options menu.

13.3 Brush Dynamics: Shape, Scattering, Texture, and More

Brush dynamics allow you to add variation and randomness to your brush strokes, making them appear more natural and organic.

Shape Dynamics:

1. **Size Jitter:** Randomly varies the size of the brush tip as you paint.
2. **Angle Jitter:** Randomly varies the angle of the brush tip.
3. **Roundness Jitter:** Randomly varies the roundness of the brush tip.
4. **Control:** Many dynamics settings have a **Control** option that allows you to specify how the variation is controlled:
   - o **Off:** No variation.
   - o **Fade:** The variation gradually decreases over a specified number of steps.
   - o **Pen Pressure:** The variation is controlled by the pressure you apply with a pressure-sensitive pen.
   - o **Pen Tilt:** The variation is controlled by the tilt angle of your pen.
   - o **Stylus Wheel:** The variation is controlled by a stylus wheel (if your pen has one).
5. **Scattering:**
6. **Scatter:** Randomly scatters the brush marks along the stroke.
7. **Both Axes:** Scatters the brush marks both horizontally and vertically.

8. **Count:** Controls the number of brush marks.
9. **Count Jitter:** Randomly varies the number of brush marks.

Texture:
- **Texture:** Applies a texture to the brush strokes.
- **Scale:** Adjusts the size of the texture.
- **Mode:** Sets the blending mode for the texture.
- **Depth:** Controls the intensity of the texture.
- **Depth Jitter:** Randomly varies the depth of the texture.

Other Dynamics:
- **Dual Brush:** Combines two brush tips to create more complex strokes.
- **Color Dynamics:** Varies the hue, saturation, brightness, and purity of the brush color as you paint.
- **Transfer:** Controls the opacity and flow of the brush with options for jitter and control.
- **Brush Pose:** This allows you to override the default behavior of your tablet's input and set it manually.
- **Noise:** Adds random noise to the brush strokes.
- **Wet Edges:** Simulates the look of wet paint building up along the edges of the brush stroke.
- **Smoothing:** Smooths out your brush strokes.

Tips for Using Brush Dynamics:
- **Experiment with different settings** to see how they affect your brush strokes.
- **Use a pressure-sensitive tablet** for the most control over brush dynamics.
- **Start with subtle variations** and gradually increase the jitter or other settings as needed.
- **Combine different dynamics** to create unique and interesting brush effects.

13.4 The Mixer Brush Tool: Simulating Real-World Painting

The Mixer Brush Tool (B) goes beyond the standard Brush Tool by simulating the behavior of traditional painting tools and techniques, such as mixing colors on a palette and loading a brush with multiple colors.

How the Mixer Brush Works:
- **Mixes Colors:** The Mixer Brush blends the colors on the canvas with the color loaded on the brush.
- **Wetness:** Controls how wet the canvas is, affecting how colors blend.
- **Load:** Determines how much paint is loaded on the brush.
- **Mix:** Controls the ratio of canvas color to brush color that is mixed.
- **Flow:** Sets the overall flow rate of the paint.

Mixer Brush Options Bar:
- **Current Brush Load:** Displays the color(s) currently loaded on the brush. Click it to open the Color Picker and choose a new color.
- **Clean Brush:** Removes paint from the brush.
- **Load Brush:** Loads the brush with the foreground color.
- **Load Solid Colors Only:** Prevents the brush from picking up colors from the canvas.
- **Clean Brush After Each Stroke:** Automatically cleans the brush after each stroke.
- **Preset Brush Settings:** Offers a variety of preset combinations of Wet, Load, Mix, and Flow settings, such as Wet, Moist, Dry, and Very Wet.
- **Wet:** Controls the wetness of the canvas.
- **Load:** Sets the amount of paint loaded on the brush.
- **Mix:** Determines the mixing ratio between the canvas color and the brush color.
- **Flow:** Controls the overall flow rate of the paint.
- **Sample All Layers:** When checked, the Mixer Brush samples colors from all visible layers.
- **Use Pen Pressure for Size:** Controls brush size with pen pressure.

Tips for Using the Mixer Brush:
- **Start with a preset brush setting** to get a feel for how the tool works.
- **Experiment with different combinations of Wet, Load, and Mix** to achieve various painting effects.

- **Use a pressure-sensitive tablet** for the most realistic painting experience.
- **Load multiple colors onto the brush** by **Alt-clicking (Windows) / Option-clicking (macOS)** on different areas of your image.
- **Clean the brush frequently** to avoid unwanted color mixing.

13.5 The Pencil Tool: For Hard-Edged Lines

The Pencil Tool (B) is similar to the Brush Tool but creates hard-edged lines with no anti-aliasing. It's useful for creating pixel art, making precise selections, or drawing crisp lines.

Pencil Tool Options Bar:
- **Brush Preset Picker:** Choose a brush tip for the Pencil Tool.
- **Mode:** Sets the blending mode.
- **Opacity:** Controls the transparency of the pencil lines.
- **Auto Erase:** When checked, painting over pixels of the foreground color with the foreground color will erase them to the background color.

Tips for Using the Pencil Tool:
- **Use the Pencil Tool for pixel art** or when you need sharp, non-anti-aliased lines.
- **Zoom in** to work on individual pixels.
- **Combine the Pencil Tool with the Shift key** to draw straight lines.

13.6 The Color Replacement Tool

The Color Replacement Tool is a specialized painting tool that allows you to replace specific colors in your image with the foreground color while preserving the texture and shading of the original.

How to Use the Color Replacement Tool:
1. **Select the Color Replacement Tool (B)**. It's grouped with the Brush Tool in the Tools Panel.
2. **Set the Foreground Color** to the color you want to use as the replacement.
3. **Adjust settings in the Options Bar:**
    - **Brush Size and Hardness:** Similar to the Brush Tool.
    - **Mode:**
        1. **Color:** Replaces the color of the sampled pixels while preserving their luminosity. This is the most common mode.
        2. **Hue:** Replaces only the hue of the sampled pixels.
        3. **Saturation:** Replaces only the saturation of the sampled pixels.
        4. **Luminosity:** Replaces only the luminosity of the sampled pixels.
    - **Limits:**
        1. **Discontiguous:** Replaces the sampled color wherever it appears under the brush.
        2. **Contiguous:** Replaces areas that are connected to each other and contain the sampled color.
        3. **Find Edges:** Similar to Contiguous but better at preserving edge sharpness.
    - **Tolerance:** Determines the range of colors that will be replaced. A higher tolerance replaces a wider range of colors.
    - **Anti-alias:** Smooths the edges of the replacement areas.
    - **Sample:**
        1. **Continuous:** Continuously samples the color under the cursor as you paint.
        2. **Once:** Samples the color only once, when you first click.
        3. **Background Swatch:** Replaces only areas that match the current background color.
4. **Paint over the areas** where you want to replace the color.
5. **Tips for Using the Color Replacement Tool:**
6. **Use a low Tolerance** to target specific colors precisely.
7. **Zoom in** to work on details.
8. **Experiment with different Modes and Limits settings** to achieve the desired effect.

9. **The Color Replacement Tool can be useful for quickly recoloring objects** or correcting color casts in specific areas.

13.7 Creating and Using Custom Brushes

Creating custom brushes is a powerful way to extend your creative possibilities in Photoshop. You can define virtually any shape or image as a brush tip and then customize its behavior using the Brush Settings panel.

Steps to Create a Custom Brush:

1. **Create or open an image** that you want to use as the basis for your brush tip. For best results, use a black and white image or convert your image to grayscale (**Image > Mode > Grayscale**). The black areas will become the opaque parts of your brush, while the white areas will be transparent.
2. **Make a selection** around the area you want to use as the brush tip. You can use any of the selection tools (e.g., Marquee, Lasso).
3. Go to **Edit > Define Brush Preset**.
4. **Give your brush a name** and click **OK**.

Customizing Your Brush:

- Open the **Brush Settings** panel (**Window > Brush Settings**).
- Select your new brush from the **Brush Tip Shape** list.

- Adjust the various settings in the Brush Settings panel to customize the brush's behavior:

  - o **Shape Dynamics:** Add variation to the size, angle, and roundness of the brush tip.
  - o **Scattering:** Scatter the brush marks along the stroke.
  - o **Texture:** Apply a texture to the brush strokes.
  - o **Dual Brush:** Combine your custom brush with another brush tip.
  - o **Color Dynamics:** Vary the color of the brush strokes.
  - o **Transfer:** Control opacity and flow variations.
  - o **And many more!**

Saving Your Custom Brush:

- In the **Brush Preset Picker**, click the gear icon and choose **New Brush Preset**. This will save your customized brush settings along with the brush tip shape.
- You can also save your custom brushes as part of a brush set (.abr file) by using the **Preset Manager** (**Edit > Presets > Preset Manager**). Choose Brushes from the Preset Type dropdown, select the brushes you want to include, and click Save Set.

Tips for Creating Custom Brushes:

- **Start with a high-resolution image** for your brush tip to ensure good quality.
- **Use a variety of shapes and textures** to create a diverse set of brushes.
- **Experiment with different Brush Settings** to achieve unique effects.
- **Organize your custom brushes into logical categories** in the Preset Manager.

13.8 Using a Graphics Tablet for Pressure Sensitivity

While you can certainly paint and draw in Photoshop using a mouse, a graphics tablet with a pressure-sensitive pen offers a much more natural and intuitive experience.

Benefits of Using a Graphics Tablet:
- **Pressure Sensitivity:** Vary the size, opacity, flow, or other brush attributes by pressing harder or lighter with the pen. This allows for much more expressive and nuanced brushwork.
- **Tilt Sensitivity:** Some tablets and pens also support tilt sensitivity, which allows you to change the angle and shape of the brush stroke by tilting the pen.
- **Ergonomics:** Using a pen can be more comfortable and ergonomic than using a mouse for extended periods.
- **Precision:** A pen offers greater precision and control than a mouse, especially for detailed work.

Setting Up a Graphics Tablet:
- **Install the tablet drivers:** Make sure you have the latest drivers installed for your specific tablet model.
- **Configure tablet settings:** Use the tablet's control panel or system preferences to customize the pen pressure, button assignments, and other settings.
- **Enable pressure sensitivity in Photoshop:** In the Brush Settings panel, make sure that the **Control** option for **Size**, **Opacity**, or other dynamics is set to **Pen Pressure** where applicable.

Popular Graphics Tablet Brands:
- **Wacom:** One of the most popular and well-regarded brands for graphics tablets. They offer a wide range of models, from entry-level to professional.
- **Huion:** A more affordable alternative to Wacom, offering good quality tablets at competitive prices.
- **XP-Pen:** Another popular brand known for its budget-friendly tablets.

Tips for Using a Graphics Tablet:
- **Practice makes perfect.** It takes some time to get used to using a pen tablet, so be patient and keep practicing.
- **Experiment with different brush settings** to find what works best for you.
- **Customize the pen buttons** to frequently used shortcuts or commands.
- **Adjust the pressure curve** in the tablet settings to fine-tune the pen's responsiveness.

13.9 Exploring AI-Generated Brushes and Textures

The field of AI is rapidly evolving, and it's starting to impact the world of digital art and design. One exciting possibility is the use of AI to generate new and unique brushes and textures.

Potential of AI in Brush and Texture Creation:
- **Generating Variations:** AI could be used to generate variations of existing brushes, creating subtle differences in shape, texture, or dynamics.
- **Creating New Brush Types:** AI could potentially create entirely new types of brushes that would be difficult or impossible to design manually.
- **Text Prompting:** Imagine being able to type in a description like "watercolor brush with rough edges and splatter" and have an AI generate a brush that matches your description.
- **Style Transfer for Brushes:** Similar to the Style Transfer Neural Filter, AI could be used to transfer the characteristics of one brush to another.

Current State:
- As of now, there aren't any widely available AI-powered tools that are fully integrated into Photoshop for creating custom brushes. However, this is an active area of research and development.
- Some third-party developers are exploring the use of AI for brush and texture generation.
- You can find AI-generated textures on various websites and marketplaces.

How You Might Use AI-Generated Brushes and Textures in the Future:

- **Expand your creative toolkit:** AI could provide you with a vast library of unique and interesting brushes and textures to use in your work.
- **Save time:** AI could automate the process of creating custom brushes, freeing you up to focus on other aspects of your art.
- **Experiment with new styles:** AI could help you explore new artistic styles and push the boundaries of your creativity.

Challenges:

- **Technical complexity:** Developing these tools requires significant expertise in AI and machine learning.
- **User interface:** Designing intuitive interfaces for creating and using AI-generated brushes will be a challenge.
- **Quality control:** Ensuring that the AI-generated brushes and textures are of high quality and meet the needs of artists.

This concludes Chapter 13! You've now gained a solid understanding of Photoshop's painting tools, including the Brush Tool, the Mixer Brush, the Pencil Tool, and the Color Replacement Tool. You've also learned about creating and customizing brushes, using graphics tablets, and the exciting potential of AI for generating new brushes and textures.

Introduction to 3D in Photoshop

Photoshop offers a set of tools and features for working with 3D models, allowing you to create basic 3D shapes, import 3D objects from other applications, manipulate them in 3D space, apply materials and textures, adjust lighting, and render 3D scenes. While Photoshop's 3D capabilities may not be as extensive as dedicated 3D modeling or rendering applications, they can still be useful for a variety of tasks, such as creating 3D mockups, adding 3D elements to your designs, and working with 3D text.

14.1 Overview of Photoshop's 3D Capabilities

Here's a summary of what you can do with 3D in Photoshop:

1. **Create basic 3D shapes:** Photoshop allows you to create simple 3D objects like cubes, spheres, cylinders, cones, and pyramids using extrusion or from presets.
2. **Create 3D text:** You can extrude text layers into 3D objects and then manipulate their shape, materials, and lighting.
3. **Import 3D models:** Photoshop supports various 3D file formats, allowing you to import models created in other 3D applications. Supported formats may include: 3D (dae), Flash 3D (fl3), Google Earth 4 (kmz), Alias (obj), Alias Wavefront (obj), U3D, and VRML (wrl).
4. **Manipulate 3D objects:** You can move, rotate, scale, and deform 3D objects in the 3D workspace.
5. **Apply materials and textures:** Photoshop offers a library of materials that you can apply to 3D objects to change their surface appearance (e.g., color, texture, reflectivity, roughness).
6. **Adjust lighting:** You can add and manipulate light sources to create different lighting effects in your 3D scenes.
7. **Render 3D scenes:** Photoshop can render your 3D scenes to create a final, high-quality image.
8. **Export 3D models:** You can export your 3D models in various formats for use in other applications.

Limitations:

1. **Simplified Toolset:** Compared to dedicated 3D applications like Blender, Maya, or 3ds Max, Photoshop's 3D toolset is relatively limited.
2. **Performance:** Working with complex 3D scenes in Photoshop can be computationally intensive and may lead to performance issues, especially on older hardware.
3. **Phasing Out:** As mentioned earlier, Adobe is gradually phasing out 3D features in Photoshop.

14.2 Creating and Importing 3D Objects

Creating Basic 3D Shapes:

- **From Presets:**
  - Go to **3D > New Mesh from Layer > Mesh Preset**.
  - Choose a preset shape from the list (e.g., Cone, Cube, Cylinder, Sphere).

- **From Extrusion:**
  - Create a 2D shape or text layer.
  - Go to **3D > New 3D Extrusion from Selected Layer**. This will extrude the 2D shape into a 3D object.

- **Importing 3D Models:**
- Go to **3D > New 3D Layer from File**.
- Select the 3D file you want to import (e.g., OBJ, DAE, KMZ).
- Photoshop will import the model into your document as a new 3D layer.

14.3 Manipulating 3D Objects in the Workspace

When you create or import a 3D object, Photoshop automatically switches to the **3D workspace**. This workspace provides specialized tools and panels for working with 3D content.

3D Workspace:

- **3D Panel:** (**Window > 3D**) Lists all the components of your 3D scene: meshes, materials, lights, and the camera.
- **Properties Panel:** (**Window > Properties**) Displays the properties and settings for the selected 3D object, material, or light.
- **Move Tool (3D Mode):** When a 3D layer is selected, the Move Tool (V) switches to 3D mode, providing controls for manipulating 3D objects.
- **Secondary View:** This allows you to view your scene from multiple angles at the same time, such as a top and perspective view. Go to **View > Show > 3D Secondary View**.

Manipulating 3D Objects with the Move Tool:

- **Select the 3D object** you want to manipulate in the 3D Panel or by clicking on it in the document window.
- **Use the 3D axes:**
  - **Red (X-axis):** Move the object horizontally.
  - **Green (Y-axis):** Move the object vertically.
  - **Blue (Z-axis):** Move the object forward and backward in 3D space.
  - **Cubes at the end of each axis:** Scale the object along that axis.
  - **Curved rotation handles:** Rotate the object around that axis.
  - **Center cube:** Move the object freely in 3D space.
  - **Square plane between two axes:** Move the object along a 2D plane.
- **Other Manipulation Options:**
- **Properties Panel:** You can also enter precise values for position, rotation, and scale in the Properties Panel.
- **Coordinates:** In the Properties Panel, adjust the coordinates of the selected object.
- **Deform:** The Properties Panel allows you to apply various deformations to 3D objects, such as twisting, bending, and tapering.

14.4 Working with 3D Text

Creating 3D text in Photoshop is a straightforward process:

1. **Create a text layer** using the Horizontal Type Tool (T).
2. **Select the text layer** in the Layers Panel.
3. Go to **3D > New 3D Extrusion from Selected Layer**.

Customizing 3D Text:
- **Properties Panel:** Use the Properties Panel to adjust the following:
  - **Extrusion Depth:** Controls how far the text is extruded.
  - **Deform:**
    - **Extrusion Taper:** Tapers the extrusion.
    - **Extrusion Twist:** Twists the extrusion around the Z-axis.
    - **Extrusion X/Y Angle:** Shears the extrusion.
    - **Bend:** Bends the extrusion around a central axis.
  - **Bevel:** Adds a beveled edge to the text. You can adjust the width, angle, and contour of the bevel.
  - **Cap:** Choose whether to have a front and/or back cap on the extrusion.

14.5 Applying Materials and Textures to 3D Objects

Materials define the surface appearance of 3D objects, controlling their color, texture, reflectivity, roughness, and other properties.

3D Panel:
- Select the **Filter by Materials** icon in the 3D Panel.

Applying Materials:
- **Select the 3D object** you want to modify in the 3D Panel.
- **In the Properties Panel, click the Material Picker** to choose from a library of preset materials.
- **Click the folder icon** next to a property in the Properties Panel (e.g., Diffuse, Specular, Illumination, Ambient, Shine, Reflection, Roughness, Bump, Opacity, Refraction) to load a texture map. This allows you to use images to control the appearance of the material.

Editing Materials:
- **Properties Panel:** Use the sliders and color swatches in the Properties Panel to adjust the various material properties.
- **Texture Maps:** You can create or edit texture maps in Photoshop or other image editing applications.

Tips for Working with Materials:

- **Experiment with different materials and settings** to achieve the desired look.
- **Use high-quality texture maps** for the best results.
- **Consider the lighting** in your scene when choosing and adjusting materials.

14.6 Lighting and Rendering 3D Scenes

Lighting plays a crucial role in creating realistic and visually appealing 3D scenes. Photoshop allows you to add and manipulate light sources to illuminate your 3D objects.

Adding Lights:
- **3D Panel:** Select the **Filter by Lights** icon. Then, click the **Add new light to scene** button at the bottom of the 3D Panel and choose a light type from the menu.
- **Light Types:**
  - **Infinite Light:** Simulates a distant light source, like the sun.
  - **Spot Light:** A directional light source, like a spotlight.
  - **Point Light:** Emits light in all directions from a single point, like a light bulb.
  - **Image Based Light:** Uses an image to define the light's color and intensity.

Manipulating Lights:
- **Select the light** you want to adjust in the 3D Panel.
- **Use the Move Tool (3D Mode)** to reposition and rotate the light.
- **Properties Panel:** Adjust the light's color, intensity, and other properties (e.g., softness, falloff) in the Properties Panel.

Rendering:
- **Rendering** is the process of generating a final, high-quality image from your 3D scene.
- Go to **3D > Render 3D Layer** to render the scene.
- **Render Settings:** You can adjust the render quality and other settings in the **Properties Panel** when Scene is selected in the 3D panel. Higher quality settings generally take longer to render.

Tips for Lighting and Rendering:
- **Use multiple light sources** to create more realistic and interesting lighting.
- **Experiment with different light types and settings.**
- **Pay attention to shadows.** Shadows are essential for creating a sense of depth and realism.
- **Consider using Image Based Lights** to add realistic reflections and ambient lighting.

Photoshop allows you to export your 3D models in various formats for use in other applications.

How to Export:

- Go to **3D > Export 3D Layer**.
- **Choose a file format** from the drop-down menu. Common options include:
  - **Collada DAE:** A widely supported format for exchanging 3D data between applications.
  - **Wavefront|OBJ:** Another popular format for 3D models.
  - **U3D:** A format for embedding 3D content in PDF files.
  - **Google Draco:** A format used for compression and transmission of 3D mesh data.
  - **glTF:** A format designed for efficient transmission and loading of 3D scenes and models.
  - **STL:** A format often used for 3D printing.
- **Adjust the export settings** as needed (these will vary depending on the chosen format).
- **Click OK** to export the model.

Tips for Exporting:

- **Choose the appropriate file format** based on your needs and the application you'll be using the model in.
- **Simplify your model before exporting** if necessary to reduce file size and improve performance in other applications.

This concludes Chapter 14. You've now been introduced to the basics of working with 3D in Photoshop, including creating and importing 3D objects, manipulating them in the 3D workspace, working with 3D text, applying materials and textures, adjusting lighting, rendering 3D scenes, and exporting 3D models. Remember that Photoshop's 3D features are being phased out, so it's important to consider alternative workflows using dedicated 3D applications if you need more advanced 3D capabilities.

Automating Tasks with Actions

Photoshop actions are a fantastic way to streamline your workflow and save time by automating repetitive tasks. An action is essentially a recorded series of steps that you can play back with a single click, automating a sequence of commands, tool operations, and other edits. This chapter will explore how to record, play, manage, and use actions effectively, including advanced techniques like conditional actions, batch processing, and droplets.

15.1 What are Actions and How Can They Save You Time?

What are Actions?

- Actions are recorded sequences of steps performed in Photoshop.
- They can include almost any command or tool operation you can perform manually.
- Actions are saved in sets (like folders) within the Actions panel.

How Can Actions Save You Time?

- **Automating Repetitive Tasks:** If you find yourself performing the same sequence of steps repeatedly (e.g., resizing images, applying adjustments, adding watermarks), you can record those steps as an action and then play it back whenever you need to, saving significant time and effort.
- **Batch Processing:** Actions can be applied to multiple files automatically using batch processing, allowing you to process entire folders of images with a single click.
- **Consistency:** Actions ensure that the same steps are applied consistently to all images, reducing the risk of errors and inconsistencies.
- **Efficiency:** By automating routine tasks, you can free up your time to focus on more creative and complex aspects of your work.
- **Sharing Workflows:** You can share actions with others, allowing them to benefit from your optimized workflows.

Examples of Tasks You Can Automate with Actions:

- Resizing and sharpening images for the web.
- Converting images to a specific file format.
- Applying a set of color adjustments or filters.
- Adding watermarks or copyright notices.
- Creating complex effects or composites.

15.2 Recording Actions: Step-by-Step Guide

The Actions Panel:

- Open the Actions panel by going to **Window > Actions**.

Steps to Record an Action:

- **Create a New Set (Optional):**
  - In the Actions panel, click the **Create new set** button (folder icon) at the bottom of the panel.
  - Give the set a descriptive name (e.g., "Web Optimization," "Image Effects"). This helps to organize your actions.

- **Create a New Action:**
  - Click the **Create new action** button (plus sign) at the bottom of the Actions panel.
  - In the New Action dialog box:
    - **Name:** Give your action a descriptive name (e.g., "Resize to 800px," "Sepia Tone").
    - **Set:** Choose the set where you want to store the action.
    - **Function Key:** (Optional) Assign a function key shortcut to the action.
    - **Color:** (Optional) Assign a color to the action for visual organization.
    - **Record:** Click the **Record** button.

- **Start Recording:**
  - From this point on, every step you perform in Photoshop will be recorded as part of the action.
  - A red circle (recording indicator) will be displayed in the Actions panel.

- **Perform the Steps You Want to Record:** Carry out the tasks you want to automate, using any commands, tools, or adjustments as needed.
- **Stop Recording:**
  - Click the **Stop playing/recording** button (square) at the bottom of the Actions panel.

Tips for Recording Actions:

- **Plan Ahead:** Before you start recording, carefully plan the steps you want to include in your action.
- **Use Descriptive Names:** Give your actions and sets clear, descriptive names so you can easily identify them later.
- **Keep Actions Modular:** It's often better to create smaller, modular actions that perform specific tasks rather than one long action that does everything. You can then combine smaller actions to create more complex workflows.
- **Insert Stop:** If you want to allow for user input during an action (e.g., to adjust a setting manually), you can insert a stop by clicking the **Insert Stop** icon in the Actions panel menu. This will pause the action and display a message to the user.
- **Toggle Dialog On/Off:** You can control whether dialog boxes for specific steps are displayed during playback. In the Actions panel, the box icon to the left of a command indicates whether its dialog will be shown (box checked) or not (box unchecked). Clicking this box toggles the setting.

15.3 Playing Actions: Automating Your Workflow

Once you've recorded an action, you can play it back to automatically apply the recorded steps to other images or layers.

How to Play an Action:
1. **Select the action** you want to play in the Actions panel.
2. **Click the Play selection button** (triangle) at the bottom of the Actions panel.

Alternative Ways to Play Actions:
- **Double-click** the action's name in the Actions panel.
- **Assign a function key shortcut** when creating or editing the action.
- **Button Mode:** In the Actions panel menu, choose **Button Mode** to display actions as buttons. You can then simply click a button to play the corresponding action.

What Happens When You Play an Action:

- Photoshop executes the recorded steps in sequence.
- If the action includes stops, it will pause and wait for user input.
- If the action includes dialog boxes that are toggled on, those dialogs will be displayed, allowing you to adjust settings.

15.4 Managing Actions: Organizing, Editing, and Deleting

Organizing Actions:
- **Sets:** Use sets to group related actions together.
- **Move Actions:** Drag and drop actions within the Actions panel to reorder them or move them between sets.
- **Color-Coding:** Assign colors to actions to visually categorize them.
- **Editing Actions:**
- **Insert Steps:** Select a step in the action, then start recording to insert new steps after the selected step.
- **Delete Steps:** Select a step and click the **Delete** icon (trash can) or press the **Delete** key.
- **Modify Steps:** Double-click a step to modify its settings (if applicable).
- **Re-record Steps:** Select a step, click the **Record again** icon in the Actions panel menu, perform the step again, and then click the **Stop** button.
- **Toggle Steps On/Off:** Click the checkmark to the left of a step to enable or disable it.

Deleting Actions:
- Select the action or set you want to delete.
- Click the **Delete** icon (trash can) at the bottom of the Actions panel or press the **Delete** key.

- You can also right-click the action and select Delete.

Saving and Loading Actions:
- **Save Actions:**
  - ○ Select the set of actions you want to save.
  - ○ Choose **Save Actions** from the Actions panel menu.
  - ○ Choose a location and name for the .atn file.
  - ○ Click **Save**.
- **Load Actions:**
  - ○ Choose **Load Actions** from the Actions panel menu.
  - ○ Select the .atn file you want to load.
  - ○ Click **Load**.

15.5 Creating Conditional Actions

Conditional actions allow you to create actions that perform different steps based on certain conditions, such as the image's dimensions, color mode, or whether a specific layer exists.

Note: Conditional actions are a more advanced feature, and the specific implementation might vary slightly depending on the version of Photoshop.

How to Create a Conditional Action:
- Start recording a new action or edit an existing one.
- Go to the Actions panel menu and choose **Insert Conditional**.
- In the Conditional Action dialog box:
  - ○ **If:** Choose the condition you want to check (e.g., Document Width, Document Height, Color Mode, Layer Exists).
  - ○ **Then:** Select the action that should be played if the condition is true.
  - ○ **Else:** (Optional) Select an action that should be played if the condition is false.

Example:
You could create a conditional action that resizes an image differently depending on whether it's in landscape or portrait orientation:
- **If:** Document Orientation is Landscape
  - ○ **Then:** Play action "Resize Landscape"
- **Else:**
  - ○ **Then:** Play action "Resize Portrait"

Use Cases for Conditional Actions:
- Applying different settings based on image size or resolution.
- Processing color and grayscale images differently.

- Performing different actions depending on the presence or absence of specific layers.

15.6 Batch Processing: Applying Actions to Multiple Files

Batch processing allows you to apply an action to a folder of images automatically, saving you a tremendous amount of time when you need to process a large number of files.

How to Batch Process:

1. Go to **File > Automate > Batch**.

2. In the Batch dialog box:

o **Play:**
   - **Set:** Choose the set containing the action you want to use.
   - **Action:** Select the specific action.

o **Source:**
   3. **Folder:** Choose the folder containing the images you want to process.
   4. **Import:** Import images from a scanner or camera.
   5. **Opened Files:** Process all currently open files in Photoshop.
   6. **Bridge:** Process files selected in Adobe Bridge.
   7. **Include All Subfolders:** Check this option to process images in subfolders as well.
   8. **Suppress File Open Options Dialogs:** Check this option to prevent dialog boxes from appearing for individual files during the batch process. This is generally recommended unless you need to adjust settings for each file.
   9. **Suppress Color Profile Warnings:** Check this option to prevent color profile warnings from interrupting the batch process.

o **Destination:**
   10. **None:** The processed images will remain open in Photoshop.
   11. **Save and Close:** The processed images will be saved and closed.
   12. **Folder:** The processed images will be saved to a specified folder. You can choose to override the action's "Save As" commands and specify a new file naming convention.

o **Errors:** Choose whether to **Stop for Errors** or **Log Errors to File**.

Tips for Batch Processing:

1. **Test your action thoroughly on a single image** before running a batch process.
2. **Back up your original images** before running a batch process, just in case something goes wrong.
3. **Use descriptive file names** to keep track of the processed images.

15.7 Using Droplets for Easy Automation

A droplet is a small, self-running application that you can create from an action. Droplets make it even easier to apply actions to files because you can simply drag and drop files or folders onto the droplet icon to process them.

How to Create a Droplet:

1. Go to **File > Automate > Create Droplet**.

2. In the Create Droplet dialog box:

   1. **Save Droplet In:** Choose a location to save the droplet.
   2. **Play:** Select the action you want the droplet to execute.

3. **Destination:** Specify where the processed files should be saved (similar to the Batch dialog box).
4. **Errors:** Choose how to handle errors.

How to Use a Droplet:

1. **Drag and drop** one or more files or a folder onto the droplet icon.
2. The droplet will launch Photoshop (if it's not already running) and apply the associated action to the files.

Tips for Using Droplets:

1. **Place droplets in convenient locations**, such as your desktop or dock, for easy access.
2. **Create different droplets for different tasks.**
3. **Droplets are a great way to share your actions with others** who may not be familiar with Photoshop.

This concludes Chapter 15. You've now learned how to use actions to automate tasks in Photoshop, from recording and playing actions to managing them effectively. You've also explored advanced techniques like conditional actions, batch processing, and droplets.

Preparing Images for Web and Print

Once you've finished editing your images in Photoshop, you'll need to prepare them for their intended output, whether it's for display on the web or for high-quality printing. This involves optimizing file size, choosing the right file format, and considering factors like resolution and color mode. This chapter will guide you through the process of preparing images for both web and print, ensuring that your images look their best in any medium.

16.1 Optimizing Images for the Web: File Size and Quality

When preparing images for the web, the goal is to find the right balance between image quality and file size. Smaller file sizes lead to faster loading times, which is crucial for a good user experience.

Key Factors Affecting File Size and Quality:

- **File Format:** Different file formats use different compression methods, resulting in varying file sizes and quality levels. Common web formats include JPEG, PNG, and GIF.
- **Image Dimensions:** The pixel dimensions of an image (e.g., 800 x 600 pixels) directly affect its file size. Larger dimensions mean more pixels and a larger file size.
- **Resolution (PPI):** While resolution (pixels per inch) is important for print, it's less relevant for web images, which are displayed based on their pixel dimensions. For web, 72 PPI is a commonly used standard, but the actual display size will depend on the user's screen resolution.
- **Compression:** JPEG compression, in particular, allows you to trade off image quality for smaller file size.
- **Color Depth:** The number of colors used in an image (e.g., 8-bit for GIF, 24-bit for JPEG) affects file size.

General Guidelines for Web Optimization:

- **Choose the Right File Format:**
  - **JPEG:** Best for photographs and images with continuous tones.
  - **PNG:** Best for graphics, logos, images with sharp lines and text, and images that require transparency.
  - **GIF:** Suitable for simple graphics with limited colors and for animations.
- **Resize Images Appropriately:** Resize your images to the actual dimensions at which they will be displayed on the web. Don't rely on HTML or CSS to resize large images, as this will still require users to download the larger file.
- **Use Compression:** When saving JPEGs, adjust the compression quality to find a good balance between file size and image quality.
- **Optimize for Mobile:** Consider the increasing use of mobile devices and optimize your images for smaller screens and potentially slower internet connections.

16.2 Using the Save for Web (Legacy) Dialog

The Save for Web (Legacy) dialog box is a powerful tool in Photoshop for optimizing images for the web. While it has been labeled "Legacy," it still offers a lot of control and remains a useful option.

Accessing Save for Web (Legacy):

- Go to **File > Export > Save for Web (Legacy)**.
- **Save for Web (Legacy) Interface:**
- **Preview Tabs:** The tabs at the top of the window (**Original, Optimized, 2-Up, 4-Up**) allow you to preview the image with different optimization settings.
- **Preset:** Choose from a variety of preset optimization settings for different file formats (JPEG, PNG, GIF).
- **File Format:** Select the desired file format.
- **Optimization Settings:** The settings available will vary depending on the chosen file format. Common settings include:
  - **Quality (JPEG):** Adjusts the compression level for JPEG images.
  - **Dither:** Simulates a wider range of colors by blending existing colors, often used with GIF and indexed-color images.
  - **Transparency:** Enables transparency for GIF and PNG images.
  - **Interlaced (PNG) / Progressive (JPEG):** Allows the image to be displayed gradually as it downloads.
  - **Colors:** Sets the number of colors to be used when exporting to GIF.
  - **Image Size:** Allows you to resize the image.
  - **Metadata:** Allows you to choose whether to include metadata (e.g., copyright information) in the optimized image.
- **Preview:** The preview window shows you how the image will look with the current settings. You can zoom in and out to examine the details.
- **File Size:** The estimated file size of the optimized image is displayed below the preview.

- **Animation:** These settings will allow you to modify playback and looping if you are working with an animated GIF.

Tips for Using Save for Web (Legacy):

- **Use the 2-Up or 4-Up views** to compare different optimization settings side-by-side.
- **Zoom in on the preview** to check for artifacts or loss of detail.
- **Experiment with different settings** to find the best balance between file size and image quality.
- **Pay attention to the estimated file size** and aim for the smallest possible size without sacrificing too much quality.

Photoshop allows you to create simple frame-by-frame animations and save them as animated GIFs for use on the web.

Creating an Animation:

- **Create each frame of your animation as a separate layer or layer group** in Photoshop.
- Open the **Timeline** panel (**Window > Timeline**).
- **Choose a Timeline Mode:**
  - **Create Frame Animation:** This is the traditional method for creating frame-by-frame animations.
  - **Create Video Timeline:** This mode is more suitable for video editing but can also be used for animation.
- **Create Frames:**
  - **Frame Animation:**
    - Click the small options menu in the top right of the Timeline panel and select **Make Frames From Layers**. This will create a separate frame for each layer or layer group.
    - Alternatively, you can create new frames manually by clicking the **Duplicates selected frames** button in the Timeline panel.
  - **Video Timeline:**
    - Add your layers to the timeline. You can adjust the duration and position of each layer on the timeline.
- **Set Frame Delay:** Click the small time indicator (e.g., 0 sec.) below each frame to set the duration for which that frame will be displayed.
- **Preview the Animation:** Click the **Play** button in the Timeline panel to preview your animation.
- **Looping Options:** Use the looping options menu (it says "Forever" by default) at the bottom of the Timeline panel to set whether the animation should loop once, forever, or a specific number of times.

Saving as an Animated GIF:
- Go to **File > Export > Save for Web (Legacy)**.
- **Choose GIF** as the file format.
- **Adjust settings:**
  - **Colors:** Reduce the number of colors to decrease the file size.
  - **Dither:** Apply dithering to simulate more colors and reduce banding.
  - **Transparency:** Enable transparency if needed.
  - **Lossy:** This option allows you to introduce some compression to reduce file size, similar to how it is applied in a JPEG image.
  - **Looping Options:** Confirm the desired looping behavior.
- **Preview the animation** in the Save for Web dialog.
- **Click Save** to save the animated GIF.

Tips for Creating Animated GIFs:
- **Keep it short and simple.** Animated GIFs are best for short, looping animations.
- **Optimize for file size.** Use a limited number of colors, reduce the frame rate if possible, and crop the image to the smallest necessary dimensions.
- **Use frame animation for simple animations** and the video timeline for more complex animations or video editing.

16.4 Preparing Images for Print: Resolution, Color Mode, and File Format

Preparing images for print requires different considerations than preparing images for the web. Print quality is paramount, and file size is less of a concern.

Key Factors for Print:
- **Resolution:** For high-quality printing, a resolution of **300 PPI** (pixels per inch) is generally recommended.
- **Color Mode:** Use **CMYK** color mode for images intended for professional printing.
- **File Format: TIFF** is often preferred for print because it supports lossless compression and can preserve layers. **PSD** is also suitable if you need to maintain layers for further editing. **JPEG** can be used if file size is a concern, but make sure to use the highest quality setting.
- **Bleed:** If your image extends to the edge of the printed page, you'll need to add a bleed area to ensure that no white edges appear after trimming. A common bleed size is 1/8 inch (0.125 inches) or 3mm. You can do this by increasing the canvas size.
- **Crop Marks:** These are lines that indicate where the printed page should be trimmed.

Steps to Prepare an Image for Print:
- **Image Size:**

- o Go to **Image > Image Size**.
- o Make sure **Resample** is checked.
- o Set the **Resolution** to 300 PPI.
- o Adjust the **Width** and **Height** to the desired print dimensions.
- o Choose an appropriate **Resampling** method (e.g., Bicubic Smoother for enlargements, Bicubic Sharper for reductions).
- **Color Mode:**
  - o Go to **Image > Mode > CMYK Color**.
  - o You may be prompted to flatten the image. If you want to preserve layers, save a copy of your document in PSD format before converting to CMYK.
- **Canvas Size (for Bleed):**
  - o If you need to add a bleed, go to **Image > Canvas Size**.
  - o Check the **Relative** box.
  - o Enter the bleed amount (e.g., 0.25 inches for both width and height for a 1/8 inch bleed on all sides).
  - o Make sure the **Anchor** is set to the center.
- **Save As:**
  - o Go to **File > Save As**.
  - o Choose **TIFF** or **PSD** as the file format.
  - o If saving as TIFF, choose appropriate compression options (LZW or ZIP are generally recommended for lossless compression).

16.5 Working with Print Service Providers

If you're sending your images to a professional print service provider (e.g., a commercial printer, a photo lab), it's essential to communicate with them to ensure that your images are prepared correctly.

Key Considerations:
- **File Format:** Ask the printer what file format they prefer (e.g., TIFF, PDF, EPS).
- **Resolution:** Confirm the required resolution (usually 300 PPI).
- **Color Mode:** Make sure your images are in the correct color mode (usually CMYK).
- **Color Profile:** Ask the printer if they have a specific color profile they recommend using.
- **Bleed and Crop Marks:** If necessary, add a bleed area and crop marks according to the printer's specifications.
- **File Naming:** Follow any specific file naming conventions required by the printer.
- **Providing Files to the Printer:**
- **File Transfer:** You might upload files to the printer's FTP server, use a file-sharing service like Dropbox or WeTransfer, or deliver the files on a physical storage device.

- **Proofing:** The printer may provide you with a proof (a printed sample) for your approval before printing the final job.

Soft proofing allows you to preview on your monitor how your image will look when printed. This can help you identify potential color issues and make adjustments before sending the image to print.

How to Soft Proof:

1. Go to **View > Proof Setup**.
2. Choose a **proof profile** from the list. This should be the color profile provided by your print service provider or a profile that closely matches the intended printing conditions (e.g., a generic CMYK profile).
3. **Gamut Warning:** (Optional) Go to **View > Gamut Warning** to highlight areas of your image that are outside the printable color gamut of the selected proof profile. These areas will be displayed in gray by default, but you can change this color in Preferences > Transparency & Gamut.

Soft Proofing Options:

- **Preserve CMYK/RGB Numbers:** This option simulates how the image will look if the color values are sent directly to the printer without any color conversion. It is generally unchecked.
- **Rendering Intent:** This determines how colors that are out of gamut are handled when converting to the proof profile:
  - **Perceptual:** Aims to preserve the overall color relationships, even if it means shifting some colors slightly. It is often a good choice for photographs.
  - **Saturation:** Tries to preserve the saturation of colors, even if it means sacrificing some accuracy in hue or lightness. It can be useful for graphics with vibrant colors.
  - **Relative Colorimetric:** Maps the white point of the source color space to the white point of the destination color space. Out-of-gamut colors are clipped to the closest reproducible color.
  - **Absolute Colorimetric:** Similar to Relative Colorimetric, but it doesn't adjust for the white point difference. This can result in a more accurate simulation of the printed output, but it may also make the image look duller on screen.
- **Black Point Compensation:** This option helps to preserve detail in the shadows when converting between color spaces. It is generally recommended to keep it checked.
- **Simulate Paper Color:** This option attempts to simulate the color of the paper on your monitor. It will only have an effect if the proof profile contains information about the paper white point.
- **Simulate Black Ink:** This option dims the blacks on your monitor to better simulate the black that will be achieved on the printed piece.

Tips for Soft Proofing:

- **Calibrate your monitor** regularly to ensure accurate color representation.

- **Use the correct proof profile** for your intended printer and paper.
- **Soft proofing is a simulation**, and there will always be some differences between what you see on your monitor and the final printed output.

16.7 Exporting with Generative AI for Enhanced Quality

This is a more forward-looking section, as the use of AI for image enhancement during export is still an emerging area. However, it's worth considering the potential possibilities.

Potential Applications of AI in Export:

- **AI-Powered Upscaling:** Similar to the Super Zoom Neural Filter, AI could be used to intelligently enlarge images during export, preserving detail and sharpness better than traditional resampling methods.
- **Artifact Reduction:** AI could help to reduce artifacts caused by compression (e.g., JPEG artifacts) or other image degradation during export.
- **Smart Sharpening:** AI could analyze the image content and apply sharpening selectively to areas that need it most, avoiding over-sharpening and noise.
- **Content-Aware Adjustments:** AI could make automatic adjustments to color, tone, and contrast during export, optimizing the image for the specific output medium (web or print).

Challenges:

- **Computational Cost:** AI-powered image processing can be computationally intensive, which could slow down the export process.
- **Quality Control:** Ensuring that AI enhancements produce consistent and desirable results across a wide range of images.
- **User Interface:** Integrating AI features into the export workflow in a user-friendly way.

Current State:

- As of now, there aren't any widely available AI features in Photoshop's export options that are as sophisticated as what's described above. However, this is an area where we can expect to see significant advancements in the coming years.
- Third-party developers are exploring the use of AI for image enhancement during export.

This concludes Chapter 16! You've now learned how to prepare your images for both web and print, including optimizing file size and quality for the web, using the Save for Web (Legacy) dialog, creating animated GIFs, and preparing images for print with the correct resolution, color mode, and file format. You've also explored how to work with print service providers and how to use soft proofing to preview your printed output.

Troubleshooting and Best Practices

Throughout this book, you've learned a wide range of Photoshop tools and techniques. Now, let's focus on some best practices and troubleshooting tips that will help you work more efficiently, avoid common problems, and get the most out of Photoshop. This chapter will cover common issues, performance optimization, keyboard shortcuts, non-destructive editing, file management, backups, and resources for further learning.

17.1 Common Photoshop Problems and How to Solve Them

Here are some of the most common problems Photoshop users encounter and their solutions:

- **Photoshop is running slowly or crashing:**
  - **Insufficient RAM:** Photoshop is a memory-intensive application. Close unnecessary programs, allocate more RAM to Photoshop in Preferences > Performance, or consider upgrading your computer's RAM.
  - **Scratch Disk Issues:** Make sure your scratch disk has enough free space (at least 20-50 GB is recommended). Consider using a dedicated, fast SSD as your scratch disk.
  - **Outdated Graphics Card Drivers:** Ensure you have the latest drivers installed for your graphics card.
  - **Too Many Layers or History States:** Reduce the number of layers if possible, merge layers when appropriate, and limit the number of History States in Preferences > Performance.
  - **Corrupted Preferences:** Try resetting Photoshop's preferences. Hold down **Ctrl+Alt+Shift (Windows) / Cmd+Option+Shift (macOS)** immediately after launching Photoshop and click "Yes" when prompted to delete the settings file.

- **Tool is not working as expected:**
  - **Check the Options Bar:** Make sure the settings for the tool are correct (e.g., blending mode, opacity, flow).
  - **Check for Selections:** An active selection can restrict the area where a tool can be applied. Go to **Select > Deselect** to clear any selections.
  - **Check the Layers Panel:** Make sure you have the correct layer selected and that it's not locked or hidden.
  - **Reset the Tool:** Right-click (Windows) or Control-click (macOS) on the tool's icon in the Options Bar and choose **Reset Tool**.

- **Image appears pixelated or blurry:**

- o **Low Resolution:** The image may have a low resolution. Check the image size (**Image > Image Size**). For print, you generally need 300 PPI. For web, 72 PPI is often sufficient, but the pixel dimensions should match the intended display size.
- o **Excessive Upsampling:** Enlarging an image too much can lead to pixelation. Try to avoid upsampling whenever possible. If you must enlarge, use a specialized image enlargement tool or AI-powered upscaling.
- o **Over-Sharpening:** Too much sharpening can create artifacts and a pixelated appearance.

- **Colors look different on different devices or in print:**
  - o **Color Management:** Make sure you're using a consistent color management workflow. Calibrate your monitor and use appropriate color profiles.
  - o **Color Mode:** Use RGB for web and screen display, and CMYK for print.
  - o **Soft Proofing:** Use soft proofing (**View > Proof Setup**) to preview how your image will look when printed.

- **File is too large:**
  - o **Reduce Image Dimensions:** Resize the image to the appropriate dimensions for its intended use.
  - o **Crop Unnecessary Areas:** Crop away any parts of the image that are not needed.
  - o **Lower Bit Depth:** If you're working with a 16-bit or 32-bit image, consider converting it to 8-bit if the higher bit depth is not necessary.
  - o **Optimize for Web:** Use the **Save for Web (Legacy)** dialog to optimize images for web use.
  - o **Flatten Layers:** If you're finished editing and don't need to preserve layers, flattening the image (**Layer > Flatten Image**) can significantly reduce file size.
  - o **Use appropriate file formats:** Choose JPEG for photographs on the web, PNG for graphics with transparency, and TIFF or PSD for high-quality print or archiving.

17.2 Performance Optimization Tips

Here are some tips to help Photoshop run faster and more smoothly:

- **Allocate Sufficient RAM:** Go to **Preferences > Performance** and adjust the "Let Photoshop Use" slider to allocate more RAM to Photoshop (70-85% is generally a good range).
- **Use a Dedicated Scratch Disk:** A fast SSD is ideal. Go to **Preferences > Scratch Disks** to configure your scratch disk settings.

- **Close Unnecessary Programs:** Free up system resources by closing other applications you're not using.
- **Purge the Cache:** Go to **Edit > Purge > All** to clear Photoshop's clipboard, histories, and video cache.
- **Limit History States:** Go to **Preferences > Performance** and reduce the number of History States if necessary.
- **Disable Unused Panels:** Close any panels you're not actively using.
- **Turn Off Font Preview:** Go to **Preferences > Type** and uncheck "Font Preview Size."
- **Optimize Image Size and Resolution:** Work with images at the appropriate size and resolution for their intended use.
- **Use Smart Objects:** Smart Objects can help to improve performance when working with multiple transformations and filters.
- **Update Photoshop:** Make sure you're using the latest version of Photoshop, as updates often include performance improvements.
- **Upgrade Your Hardware:** If you regularly work with large, complex files, consider upgrading your computer's RAM, processor, and graphics card.

17.3 Keyboard Shortcuts for Efficient Workflow

Learning keyboard shortcuts can dramatically speed up your workflow in Photoshop. Here are some of the most useful shortcuts:

Basic Shortcuts:
- **Ctrl+N (Windows) / Cmd+N (macOS):** New Document
- **Ctrl+O / Cmd+O:** Open
- **Ctrl+S / Cmd+S:** Save
- **Ctrl+Shift+S / Cmd+Shift+S:** Save As
- **Ctrl+Z / Cmd+Z:** Undo
- **Ctrl+Shift+Z / Cmd+Shift+Z:** Redo
- **Ctrl+A / Cmd+A:** Select All
- **Ctrl+D / Cmd+D:** Deselect
- **Ctrl+T / Cmd+T:** Free Transform
- **Ctrl+J / Cmd+J:** Duplicate Layer
- **Ctrl+G / Cmd+G:** Group Layers
- **Ctrl+E / Cmd+E:** Merge Layers
- **Ctrl + "+" / Cmd + "+":** Zoom In
- **Ctrl + "-" / Cmd + "-":** Zoom Out
- **Spacebar:** Temporarily access the Hand Tool to pan around the image.

Tool Shortcuts:
- **V:** Move Tool
- **M:** Marquee Tools
- **L:** Lasso Tools
- **W:** Magic Wand, Quick Selection Tool
- **C:** Crop Tool
- **I:** Eyedropper Tool
- **J:** Spot Healing Brush, Healing Brush, Patch Tool, Content-Aware Move Tool, Red Eye Tool
- **B:** Brush Tool, Pencil Tool, Color Replacement Tool, Mixer Brush Tool
- **S:** Clone Stamp Tool, Pattern Stamp Tool
- **Y:** History Brush Tool, Art History Brush Tool
- **E:** Eraser Tool
- **G:** Gradient Tool, Paint Bucket Tool
- **O:** Dodge Tool, Burn Tool, Sponge Tool
- **P:** Pen Tool
- **T:** Type Tool
- **A:** Path Selection Tool, Direct Selection Tool
- **U:** Shape Tools
- **H:** Hand Tool
- **R:** Rotate View Tool
- **Z:** Zoom Tool

Brush Tool Shortcuts:
- **[and]:** Decrease/Increase brush size
- **Shift+[and Shift+]:** Decrease/Increase brush hardness
- **1, 2, 3...0:** Change brush opacity in 10% increments (e.g., 1 = 10%, 5 = 50%, 0 = 100%)
- **Shift + 1, 2, 3...0:** Change brush flow in 10% increments
- **Panel Shortcuts:**
- **F7:** Show/Hide Layers Panel
- **F5:** Show/Hide Brush Panel
- **Ctrl+Shift+N / Cmd+Shift+N:** New Layer

Customizing Shortcuts:
You can customize Photoshop's keyboard shortcuts by going to **Edit > Keyboard Shortcuts**.

17.4 Non-Destructive Editing: Best Practices

Non-destructive editing is a crucial workflow in Photoshop that allows you to make changes to your images without permanently altering the original pixel data. This provides flexibility, allows for easier revisions, and helps to preserve image quality.

Key Principles of Non-Destructive Editing:
- **Use Adjustment Layers:** Instead of applying adjustments directly to a layer (**Image > Adjustments**), use adjustment layers (**Layer > New Adjustment**

Layer). Adjustment layers apply effects non-destructively and can be edited, masked, or deleted at any time.

- **Use Smart Objects:** Convert layers to Smart Objects before applying transformations or filters. This allows you to edit the transformations and filter settings non-destructively.
- **Use Layer Masks:** Instead of erasing pixels, use layer masks to hide or reveal parts of a layer.
- **Use Smart Filters:** When working with Smart Objects, filters are automatically applied as Smart Filters, which are editable and non-destructive.
- **Duplicate Layers:** When in doubt, duplicate a layer before making significant changes. This way, you always have a backup of the original.
- **Use the History Panel:** The History Panel allows you to step back through your edits and revert to previous states. However, it's not a substitute for a truly non-destructive workflow, as the history states are lost when you close the document.

17.5 Staying Organized: File Management and Naming Conventions

Maintaining an organized file system and using clear naming conventions are essential for efficient workflow, especially when working on complex projects or collaborating with others.

File Management:

- **Create a logical folder structure:** Organize your projects into folders and subfolders that make sense to you.

- **Use a consistent naming convention:** Use descriptive file names that clearly indicate the contents of each file. Include information like project name, date, version number, and a brief description of the image. For example:
  - ProjectName_Date_Version_Description.psd
  - AcmeCorp_2023-10-27_v03_WebsiteBanner.jpg

- **Regularly delete unnecessary files:** This will help to keep your projects manageable and prevent clutter.

Layer Organization in Photoshop:

- **Name your layers:** Give each layer a descriptive name that indicates its content (e.g., "Background," "Sky," "Portrait," "Text").
- **Group related layers:** Use layer groups to organize your Layers Panel and make it easier to navigate.
- **Color-code layers and groups:** Assign colors to layers and groups to visually categorize them.
- **Delete or hide unused layers:** Keep your Layers Panel tidy by deleting or hiding layers that you no longer need.

17.6 Backing Up Your Work

Regularly backing up your work is crucial to prevent data loss in case of hardware failure, software crashes, or accidental deletion.

Backup Strategies:

- **Multiple Backups:** Use at least two different backup methods (e.g., external hard drive, cloud storage).
- **Regular Backups:** Back up your work frequently, ideally at least once a day if you're working on an important project.
- **Automated Backups:** Use backup software or cloud services that automatically back up your files on a schedule.
- **Version Control:** Consider using a version control system (like Git) for complex projects or when collaborating with others. This allows you to track changes, revert to previous versions, and merge different versions of a file.
- **Offsite Backups:** Store at least one backup copy in a separate physical location from your computer, in case of fire, theft, or natural disaster.

Popular Backup Options:

- **External Hard Drives:** A relatively inexpensive and reliable way to back up large amounts of data.
- **Cloud Storage:** Services like Dropbox, Google Drive, iCloud, and OneDrive offer convenient online backups and file syncing.
- **Network Attached Storage (NAS):** A dedicated storage device connected to your network, providing centralized backups for multiple computers.
- **Time Machine (macOS):** A built-in backup utility for macOS that automatically backs up your entire system to an external hard drive.
- **Backup Software:** Various third-party backup applications are available for both Windows and macOS, offering more advanced features and customization options.

17.7 Resources for Further Learning

Photoshop is a vast and complex application, and there's always more to learn. Here are some excellent resources for continuing your Photoshop education:

Official Adobe Resources:

- **Adobe Photoshop User Guide:** The official documentation for Photoshop, providing comprehensive information on all features and tools.
- **Adobe Creative Cloud Learn:** A vast library of tutorials, courses, and articles on Photoshop and other Creative Cloud applications.
- **Adobe Support Community:** A forum where you can ask questions, get help from other users, and find solutions to common problems.
- **Adobe Blog:** Provides news, updates, and inspiration related to Photoshop and other Adobe products.

Online Learning Platforms:
- **LinkedIn Learning (formerly Lynda.com):** Offers a wide range of Photoshop courses for all skill levels.
- **Skillshare:** A platform with many project-based Photoshop tutorials.
- **Udemy:** Another popular online learning platform with numerous Photoshop courses.
- **CreativeLive:** Offers in-depth courses and workshops on various creative topics, including Photoshop.
- **YouTube:** A vast resource for free Photoshop tutorials, tips, and tricks. Search for specific topics or follow channels dedicated to Photoshop education.

Websites and Blogs:
- **Photoshop Cafe:** Offers tutorials, articles, and resources for Photoshop users.
- **Phlearn:** Provides high-quality Photoshop tutorials, often with a focus on photography.
- **Tuts+ (Envato):** A comprehensive resource for tutorials on various design and development topics, including Photoshop.

Keyboard Shortcuts

Keyboard shortcuts can significantly speed up your workflow in Photoshop by allowing you to quickly access tools, commands, and features without using the mouse. This appendix provides a list of some of the most useful Photoshop shortcuts, categorized by type. It also explains how to customize shortcuts to fit your preferences.

Note: The shortcuts listed below are for **Windows**. For **macOS**, substitute **Cmd** for **Ctrl** and **Option** for **Alt** in most cases.

Menu Shortcuts

These shortcuts involve accessing commands found in the menus at the top of the Photoshop interface. Many menu shortcuts require multiple keys to be pressed in sequence, not simultaneously. For example, Alt, F, S to Save As means that you should press and release Alt, then press and release F, then press and release S.

File Menu (Alt+F):
- New: Ctrl+N
- Open: Ctrl+O
- Browse in Bridge: Alt+Ctrl+O
- Open As: Alt+Shift+Ctrl+O
- Open as Smart Object: Alt, F, M
- Open Recent: Alt, F, R
- Close: Ctrl+W
- Close All: Alt+Ctrl+W

- Close and Go to Bridge: Shift+Ctrl+W
- Save: Ctrl+S
- Save As: Shift+Ctrl+S
- Revert: F12
- Export:
    - Export As: Alt+Shift+Ctrl+W
    - Save for Web (Legacy): Alt+Shift+Ctrl+S
- Generate: Alt, F, G
- Share: Alt, F, H
- Share on Behance: Alt, F, N
- Search Adobe Stock: Alt, F, K
- Place Embedded: Alt, F, B
- Place Linked: Alt, F, L
- Package: Alt, F, C

- Automate:

    1. Batch: Alt, F, A, B
    2. Create Droplet: Alt, F, A, D
    3. Conditional Mode Change: Alt, F, A, M
    4. Contact Sheet II: Alt, F, A, N
    5. Fit Image: Alt, F, A, F
    6. Lens Correction: Shift+Ctrl+R
    7. Merge to HDR Pro: Alt, F, A, G
    8. Photomerge: Alt, F, A, O
    9. PDF Presentation: Alt, F, A,

    - Scripts: Alt, F, S
    - File Info: Alt+Shift+Ctrl+I
    - Print: Ctrl+P
    - Print One Copy: Alt+Shift+Ctrl+P
    - Exit: Ctrl+Q

Edit Menu (Alt+E):
- Undo: Ctrl+Z
- Step Forward: Shift+Ctrl+Z
- Step Backward: Alt+Ctrl+Z
- Fade: Shift+Ctrl+F
- Cut: Ctrl+X
- Copy: Ctrl+C
- Copy Merged: Shift+Ctrl+C
- Paste: Ctrl+V
- Paste Special: Alt, E, S
    - Paste in Place: Shift+Ctrl+V
    - Paste Into: Alt+Shift+Ctrl+V
    - Paste Outside: Alt, E, S, O
- Clear: Del
- Check Spelling: Alt, E, C

- Find and Replace Text: Alt, E, F
- Fill: Shift+F5
- Stroke: Alt, E, S
- Content-Aware Scale: Alt+Shift+Ctrl+C
- Puppet Warp: Alt, E, W
- Perspective Warp: Alt, E, V
- Free Transform: Ctrl+T
- Transform: Alt, E, T
    - Again: Shift+Ctrl+T
    - Scale: Alt, E, T, S
    - Rotate: Alt, E, T, R
    - Skew: Alt, E, T, K
    - Distort: Alt, E, T, I
    - Perspective: Alt, E, T, V
    - Warp: Alt, E, T, W
    - Rotate 180: Alt, E, T, 1
    - Rotate 90 CW: Alt, E, T, 9
    - Rotate 90 CCW: Alt, E, T, O
    - Flip Horizontal: Alt, E, T, H
    - Flip Vertical: Alt, E, T, F
- Auto-Align Layers: Alt, E, L
- Auto-Blend Layers: Alt, E, B
- Define Brush Preset: Alt, E, D
- Define Pattern: Alt, E, N
- Define Custom Shape: Alt, E, M
- Purge: Alt, E, U
- Adobe PDF Presets: Alt, E, A
- Preset Manager: Alt, E, R
- Color Settings: Shift+Ctrl+K
- Assign Profile: Alt, E, P
- Convert to Profile: Alt, E, I
- Keyboard Shortcuts: Alt+Shift+Ctrl+K
- Menus: Alt+Shift+Ctrl+M
- Toolbar: Alt, E, B
- Workspaces: Alt, E, W

Image Menu (Alt+I):
- Mode: Alt, I, M
- Adjustments: Alt, I, A
    - Levels: Ctrl+L
    - Auto Tone: Shift+Ctrl+L
    - Auto Contrast: Alt+Shift+Ctrl+L
    - Auto Color: Shift+Ctrl+B
    - Curves: Ctrl+M
    - Exposure: Alt, I, A, E
    - Vibrance: Alt, I, A, V
    - Hue/Saturation: Ctrl+U

- o Color Balance: Ctrl+B
- o Black & White: Alt+Shift+Ctrl+B
- o Photo Filter: Alt, I, A, P
- o Channel Mixer: Alt, I, A, X
- o Color Lookup: Alt, I, A, C
- o Invert: Ctrl+I
- o Posterize: Alt, I, A, R
- o Threshold: Alt, I, A, T
- o Gradient Map: Alt, I, A, G
- o Selective Color: Alt, I, A, S
- Shadows/Highlights: Alt, I, A, W
- HDR Toning: Alt, I, A, H
- Desaturate: Shift+Ctrl+U
- Match Color: Alt, I, A, M
- Replace Color: Alt, I, A, L
- Equalize: Alt, I, A, Q
- Image Size: Alt+Ctrl+I
- Canvas Size: Alt+Ctrl+C
- Pixel Aspect Ratio: Alt, I, P
- Rotate Canvas: Alt, I, R
- Crop: Alt, I, O
- Trim: Alt, I, M
- Reveal All: Alt, I, V
- Duplicate: Alt, I, U
- Apply Image: Alt, I, Y
- Calculations: Alt, I, C
- Variables: Alt, I, B
- Analysis: Alt, I, N

Layer Menu (Alt+L):
- New: Alt, L, N
  - o Layer: Shift+Ctrl+N
  - o Layer via Copy: Ctrl+J
  - o Layer via Cut: Shift+Ctrl+J
  - o Background from Layer: Alt, L, N, B
- Duplicate Layer: Alt, L, D
- Delete: Alt, L, E
- Rename Layer: Alt, L, R
- Layer Style: Alt, L, Y
- New Fill Layer: Alt, L, F
- New Adjustment Layer: Alt, L, J
- Edit Adjustment: Alt, L, E
- Change Layer Content: Alt, L, G
- Layer Content Options: Alt, L, T
- Type: Alt, L, P
- Rasterize: Alt, L, Z
- New Layer Based Slice: Alt, L, I

- Group Layers: Ctrl+G
- Ungroup Layers: Shift+Ctrl+G
- Hide Layers: Alt, L, H
- Arrange: Alt, L, A
- Align: Alt, L, G
- Distribute: Alt, L, B
- Lock Layers: Alt, L, O
- Link Layers: Alt, L, K
- Select Linked Layers: Alt, L, C
- Merge Layers: Ctrl+E
- Merge Visible: Shift+Ctrl+E
- Flatten Image: Alt, L, N
- Matting: Alt, L, M

Type Menu (Alt+Y):
- Create Work Path: Alt, Y, W
- Convert to Shape: Alt, Y, V
- Rasterize Type Layer: Alt, Y, R
- Create 3D Extrusion: Alt, Y, X
- Warp Text: Alt, Y, P
- Convert to Paragraph Text: Alt, Y, H
- Update All Text Layers: Alt, Y, U
- Replace All Missing Fonts: Alt, Y, M
- Resolve Missing Fonts: Alt, Y, F
- Paste Lorem Ipsum: Alt, Y, L
- Load Type Styles: Alt, Y, S
- Save Type Styles: Alt, Y, T
- Font Preview Size: Alt, Y, Z
- Anti-Alias: Alt, Y, A
- Orientation: Alt, Y, O
- OpenType: Alt, Y, Y
- Language Options: Alt, Y, G
- Panels: Alt, Y, E

Select Menu (Alt+S):
- All: Ctrl+A
- Deselect: Ctrl+D
- Reselect: Shift+Ctrl+D
- Inverse: Shift+Ctrl+I
- All Layers: Alt+Ctrl+A
- Deselect Layers: Alt, S, Y
- Find Layers: Alt, S, F
- Isolate Layers: Alt, S, I
- Color Range: Alt, S, C
- Focus Area: Alt, S, U
- Subject: Alt, S, B
- Sky: Alt, S, K

- Select and Mask: Alt+Ctrl+R
- Modify: Alt, S, M
- Grow: Alt, S, G
- Similar: Alt, S, I
- Transform Selection: Alt, S, T
- Edit in Quick Mask Mode: Alt, S, Q
- Load Selection: Alt, S, L
- Save Selection: Alt, S, V

Filter Menu (Alt+T):
- Last Filter: Ctrl+F
- Convert for Smart Filters: Alt, T, V
- Adaptive Wide Angle: Alt+Shift+Ctrl+A
- Camera Raw Filter: Shift+Ctrl+A
- Lens Correction: Shift+Ctrl+R
- Liquify: Shift+Ctrl+X
- Vanishing Point: Alt+Ctrl+V
- 3D: Alt, T, D
- Blur: Alt, T, B
- Blur Gallery: Alt, T, G
- Distort: Alt, T, I
- Noise: Alt, T, N
- Pixelate: Alt, T, P
- Render: Alt, T, R
- Sharpen: Alt, T, H
- Stylize: Alt, T, Y
- Video: Alt, T, D
- Other: Alt, T, O
- Digimarc: Alt, T, M

View Menu (Alt+V):
- Proof Setup: Alt, V, F
- Proof Colors: Ctrl+Y
- Gamut Warning: Shift+Ctrl+Y
- Zoom In: Ctrl++
- Zoom Out: Ctrl+-
- Fit on Screen: Ctrl+0
- 100%: Ctrl+1
- 200%: Alt, V, 2
- Print Size: Alt, V, P
- Screen Mode: Alt, V, S
- Extras: Ctrl+H
- Show: Alt, V, W
- Rulers: Ctrl+R
- Snap: Shift+Ctrl+;
- Snap To: Alt, V, T
- Lock Guides: Alt+Ctrl+;

- Clear Guides: Alt, V, C
- New Guide: Alt, V, N
- New Guide Layout: Alt, V, Y
- Lock Slices: Alt, V, I
- Clear Slices: Alt, V, L
- 3D: Alt, V, 3

Window Menu (Alt+W):

- Arrange: Alt, W, A
- Workspace: Alt, W, W
- Extensions: Alt, W, X
- Application Frame: Alt, W, F
- Application Bar: Alt, W, B
- Options: Alt, W, O
- Tools: Alt, W, T
- Adjustments: Alt, W, J
- Brush Settings: F5
- Brushes: Alt, W, U
- Channels: Alt, W, H
- Character: Alt, W, C
- Character Styles: Alt, W, Y
- Clone Source: Alt, W, L
- Color: F6
- Histogram: Alt, W, I
- History: Alt, W, S
- Info: F8
- Layer Comps: Alt, W, M
- Layers: F7
- Paths: Alt, W, P
- Properties: Alt, W, R
- Swatches: Alt, W, E

Tool Shortcuts

- **Move Tool:** V
- **Marquee Tools:** M (Rectangular, Elliptical, Single Row, Single Column)
- **Lasso Tools:** L (Lasso, Polygonal Lasso, Magnetic Lasso)
- **Object Selection, Quick Selection, Magic Wand Tool:** W
- **Crop Tool:** C (Crop, Perspective Crop, Slice, Slice Select)
- **Frame Tool:** K
- **Eyedropper Tool:** I (Eyedropper, 3D Material Eyedropper, Color Sampler, Ruler, Note, Count)
- **Spot Healing Brush Tool:** J (Spot Healing Brush, Healing Brush, Patch, Content-Aware Move, Red Eye)
- **Brush Tool:** B (Brush, Pencil, Color Replacement, Mixer Brush)
- **Clone Stamp Tool:** S (Clone Stamp, Pattern Stamp)
- **History Brush Tool:** Y (History Brush, Art History Brush)
- **Eraser Tool:** E (Eraser, Background Eraser, Magic Eraser)
- **Gradient Tool:** G (Gradient, Paint Bucket, 3D Material Drop)
- **Dodge Tool:** O (Dodge, Burn, Sponge)
- **Pen Tool:** P (Pen, Freeform Pen, Curvature Pen, Add Anchor Point, Delete Anchor Point, Convert Point)
- **Type Tool:** T (Horizontal Type, Vertical Type, Horizontal Type Mask, Vertical Type Mask)

Panel Shortcuts

- **Actions:** F9 (or Alt+F9 if not in Button Mode)
- **Adjustments:** Alt+Shift+Ctrl+J
- **Brush Settings:** F5
- **Brushes:** Alt+Shift+Ctrl+U
- **Channels:** Alt+Shift+Ctrl+H
- **Character:** Ctrl+T
- **Character Styles:** Alt+Shift+Ctrl+Y
- **Clone Source:** Alt+Shift+Ctrl+L
- **Color:** F6
- **Histogram:** Alt+Shift+Ctrl+I
- **History:** Alt+F9
- **Info:** F8
- **Layer Comps:** Alt+Shift+Ctrl+M
- **Layers:** F7
- **Measurement Log:** Alt+Shift+Ctrl+G
- **Notes:** Alt+Shift+Ctrl+N
- **Paragraph:** Alt+Ctrl+T
- **Paragraph Styles:** Alt+Shift+Ctrl+R
- **Paths:** Alt+Shift+Ctrl+P
- **Properties:** Alt+Shift+Ctrl+E
- **Swatches:** Alt+Shift+Ctrl+E

- **Timeline:** Alt+Shift+Ctrl+K
- **Tool Presets:** Alt+Shift+Ctrl+Y

Filter Shortcuts

- **Last Filter:** Ctrl+F
- **Adaptive Wide Angle:** Alt+Shift+Ctrl+A
- **Camera Raw Filter:** Shift+Ctrl+A
- **Lens Correction:** Shift+Ctrl+R
- **Liquify:** Shift+Ctrl+X
- **Vanishing Point:** Alt+Ctrl+V

Note: Many individual filters within the Filter Gallery or submenus under the Filter menu do not have default keyboard shortcuts. However, you can assign custom shortcuts to them (see "Customizing Shortcuts" below).

Customizing Shortcuts

Photoshop allows you to customize keyboard shortcuts to fit your individual workflow and preferences.

How to Customize Shortcuts:

1. Go to **Edit > Keyboard Shortcuts** or use the shortcut **Alt+Shift+Ctrl+K**.
2. The **Keyboard Shortcuts and Menus** dialog box will open.
3. **Choose a Set:** You can create a new set of shortcuts or modify the default set (Photoshop Defaults).
4. **Select the Type of Shortcuts:**
   - **Application Menus:** Shortcuts for commands found in the menus.
   - **Panel Menus:** Shortcuts for commands found in panel menus.
   - **Tools:** Shortcuts for selecting tools in the Tools Panel.
5. **Find the Command or Tool:** Expand the appropriate category (e.g., File, Edit, Image, Layer, Select, Filter, View, Window, Help, or the specific tool category).
6. **Assign a Shortcut:**
   - Click in the **Shortcut** column next to the command or tool you want to modify.
   - Press the desired key combination.
   - If the shortcut is already in use, Photoshop will display a warning. You can choose to override the existing shortcut or try a different combination.
7. **Accept Changes:** Click the **Accept** button to apply the changes to the current shortcut, then click **OK** to close the dialog box.

Tips for Customizing Shortcuts:
- **Create a new set** to store your custom shortcuts. This way, you can easily switch between your custom set and the default Photoshop shortcuts.
- **Use memorable and logical shortcuts** that are easy for you to remember.
- **Avoid conflicts** with common operating system shortcuts.
- **Don't be afraid to experiment** and find what works best for you.

- **You can export your custom shortcut sets** as .kys files to share with others or to use on a different computer.

This concludes Keyboard Shortcuts. By mastering these shortcuts and customizing them to your liking, you can significantly speed up your Photoshop workflow and work more efficiently.

Glossary of Terms

This glossary provides definitions for common terms used in Adobe Photoshop and throughout this book.

- **8-bit, 16-bit, 32-bit:** Refer to the bit depth of an image, which determines the amount of color information stored for each pixel. Higher bit depths allow for more colors and smoother gradations.
- **Actions:** Recorded sequences of steps in Photoshop that can be played back to automate tasks.
- **Adjustment Layer:** A special type of layer that applies non-destructive color and tonal adjustments to the layers below it.
- **Alpha Channel:** A grayscale channel that stores selection information. Often used for saving and loading selections.
- **Aliasing:** The jagged or stair-stepped appearance of diagonal lines or curves in a digital image, caused by insufficient resolution.
- **Anti-aliasing:** A technique used to smooth the edges of objects, including text, by partially filling in pixels along the edge.
- **Artboard:** A separate canvas within a Photoshop document. Useful for designing for multiple screens or creating variations of a design.
- **Aspect Ratio:** The proportional relationship between the width and height of an image.
- **Batch Processing:** Applying an action or a series of commands to multiple files automatically.
- **Bevel:** A 3D effect that makes an object appear raised or indented by simulating beveled edges.
- **Bit Depth:** The number of bits used to represent the color of a single pixel. Common bit depths are 8-bit (256 colors per channel), 16-bit (65,536 colors per channel), and 32-bit (over 4 billion colors per channel).
- **Bitmap:** See **Raster Graphics**.
- **Blend If:** A feature in the Layer Style dialog that allows you to create masks based on the luminosity of the current layer or the underlying layers.
- **Blending Mode:** Determines how a layer's pixels blend with the pixels in the layers below it. Examples include Normal, Multiply, Screen, Overlay, and many more.
- **BMP:** A standard Windows image format that supports various color depths.
- **Brightness:** The overall lightness or darkness of an image or a specific area.
- **Brush Dynamics:** Settings that control variations in brush stroke characteristics, such as size, angle, roundness, and color, often controlled by pen pressure, tilt, or other inputs.
- **Brush Preset:** A saved set of brush settings, including the brush tip shape, size, hardness, and other options.
- **Canvas:** The working area in Photoshop where you create and edit images.
- **Canvas Size:** The dimensions of the entire working area (canvas) in Photoshop.

- **Channel:** A grayscale representation of a specific color component in an image. For example, an RGB image has separate channels for red, green, and blue.
- **Clipping:** Loss of image detail due to tonal values that are outside the range that can be represented by the image's bit depth or the output device. Can occur in shadows (shadow clipping) or highlights (highlight clipping).
- **Clipping Mask:** A layer or group whose shape or transparency masks the layers above it, confining their visibility to the shape or transparency of the base layer.
- **Clone:** To duplicate pixels from one area of an image to another using the Clone Stamp Tool.
- **CMYK:** A subtractive color model used for print, based on the colors Cyan, Magenta, Yellow, and Key (black).
- **Color Balance:** The relative amounts of different colors in an image. Also, an adjustment tool in Photoshop for correcting color casts.
- **Color Cast:** An unwanted overall tint or hue in an image, often caused by lighting conditions.
- **Color Gamut:** The range of colors that a particular device (e.g., monitor, printer) or color space can reproduce.
- **Color Management:** A system for ensuring accurate and consistent color reproduction across different devices.
- **Color Mode:** Determines how colors are represented in a digital image (e.g., RGB, CMYK, Grayscale, Lab).
- **Color Profile:** A set of data that describes the color characteristics of a device or color space.
- **Color Space:** A specific range of colors that can be represented by a color model. Examples include sRGB, Adobe RGB, and ProPhoto RGB.
- **Compositing:** The process of combining elements from multiple images into a single image.
- **Compression:** A method for reducing the file size of an image. Compression can be lossy (some data is discarded) or lossless (no data is lost).
- **Content-Aware:** A technology in Photoshop that uses AI to intelligently fill in, move, or scale areas of an image based on the surrounding content.
- **Contrast:** The difference between the light and dark areas of an image.
- **Crop:** To remove unwanted portions of an image.
- **Curves:** An advanced tool for adjusting the tonal range and contrast of an image by manipulating a curve that represents the relationship between input and output levels.
- **Desaturate:** To decrease the intensity of colors in an image, making them closer to gray.
- **Diffusion:** In the context of brushes, refers to how quickly the pasted pixels from the healing brush or clone stamp are adapted to their surroundings. In the context of dithering, it refers to how colors are mixed to simulate a wider range of colors.
- **Dithering:** A technique used to simulate a wider range of colors by intermingling pixels of different colors, often used when saving images in formats with limited color palettes (e.g., GIF).

- **Dodge:** To lighten specific areas of an image using the Dodge Tool.
- **DPI (Dots Per Inch):** A measure of printer resolution, indicating the number of ink dots a printer can place per inch.
- **Droplet:** A small, self-running application created from a Photoshop action that allows for easy batch processing by dragging and dropping files onto it.
- **Duotone:** An image that uses two colors, often for artistic effect.
- **EPS (Encapsulated PostScript):** A vector file format often used for logos and illustrations.
- **Exposure:** The amount of light that reaches the camera sensor or film. In Photoshop, Exposure is also an adjustment tool for correcting overexposed or underexposed images.
- **Feather:** To soften the edges of a selection or an image by creating a gradual transition zone.
- **File Format:** The way in which image data is stored (e.g., JPEG, PNG, TIFF, GIF, PSD).
- **Filter:** A tool or command that applies a specific effect to an image or layer, such as blurring, sharpening, stylizing, or distorting.
- **Filter Gallery:** A central location in Photoshop for accessing and applying a wide range of filters.
- **Flow:** A brush setting that controls the rate at which paint is applied.
- **Foreground Color:** The color that is currently selected for painting, drawing, or filling.
- **Frequency Separation:** An advanced retouching technique that involves separating an image into high-frequency (detail) and low-frequency (color and tone) layers.
- **Gamut Warning:** A feature that highlights areas of an image that are outside the printable color gamut of a selected color profile.
- **GIF (Graphics Interchange Format):** A raster image format commonly used for web graphics, especially those with limited colors or animation. Supports transparency but only 256 colors.
- **Gradient:** A gradual blend between two or more colors.
- **Grayscale:** An image that only contains shades of gray, from black to white.
- **Guides:** Non-printing lines that can be placed on the canvas to help with alignment and layout.
- **Healing Brush:** A retouching tool that blends the texture from a sampled area with the color and luminosity of the area being repaired.
- **High Dynamic Range (HDR):** An imaging technique that captures or simulates a wider range of brightness levels than standard images, often used to create images with greater detail in both highlights and shadows.
- **Histogram:** A graph that shows the tonal distribution in an image, representing the number of pixels at each brightness level.
- **History Panel:** A panel that records the recent editing steps performed on an image, allowing you to undo or redo actions or revert to a previous state.
- **Hue:** The pure color or shade, such as red, green, or blue.
- **Image Size:** The dimensions of an image, usually expressed in pixels.
- **Interpolation:** The process of generating new pixels when resizing an image. See also **Resampling**.

- **JPEG (Joint Photographic Experts Group):** A common raster image format that uses lossy compression, making it suitable for photographs and web images.
- **Kerning:** The adjustment of space between two specific characters of text.
- **Layer:** A separate element within a Photoshop document that can contain images, text, shapes, or adjustments. Layers are stacked on top of each other to create the composite image.
- **Layer Mask:** A grayscale image associated with a layer that is used to control the layer's transparency. White areas reveal, black areas conceal, and gray areas create partial transparency.
- **Layer Style:** Non-destructive effects that can be applied to a layer, such as drop shadows, glows, bevels, and strokes.
- **Leading:** The vertical space between lines of text.
- **Levels:** A tool for adjusting the tonal range and color balance of an image by manipulating the distribution of shadows, midtones, and highlights.
- **Liquify:** A filter that allows you to push, pull, rotate, reflect, pucker, and bloat the pixels of an image.
- **Lossless Compression:** A compression method that reduces file size without discarding any image data.
- **Lossy Compression:** A compression method that reduces file size by discarding some image data, potentially resulting in a loss of quality.
- **Luminosity:** The brightness or lightness of a color or an area of an image.
- **Marching Ants:** The animated dotted line that indicates an active selection in Photoshop.
- **Marquee:** A selection tool used to create rectangular, elliptical, single-row, or single-column selections.
- **Mask:** A way to isolate and protect parts of an image from changes.
- **Material:** In 3D modeling, a set of properties that define the surface appearance of a 3D object.
- **Midtones:** The tones in an image that fall between the highlights and shadows.
- **Mixer Brush:** A painting tool that simulates the behavior of traditional painting tools, including mixing colors on the canvas and loading the brush with multiple colors.
- **Moiré:** An undesirable pattern that can appear when scanning or photographing images with repeating patterns, such as textiles or screen prints.
- **Neural Filters:** AI-powered filters in Photoshop that can perform complex image transformations, such as skin smoothing, style transfer, and colorization.
- **Noise:** Random variations in pixel color or brightness that can make an image appear grainy.
- **Non-Destructive Editing:** A workflow that preserves the original image data and allows for changes to be made without permanently altering the underlying pixels.
- **Opacity:** The degree to which an object or layer is transparent or opaque.
- **Options Bar:** A context-sensitive bar located below the Menu Bar that displays options and settings for the currently selected tool.

- **ಪ್ಯಾಚ್ ಟೂಲ್:** A retouching tool that allows you to select an area you want to repair and then drag that selection to a source area to sample from, blending the texture and color to create a seamless patch.
- **Path:** A vector outline that can be used to create selections, shapes, or guide text.
- **Pattern:** A repeating design that can be used to fill areas or create textures.
- **Pen Tool:** A tool for creating and editing vector paths.
- **Perspective:** The way in which objects appear to get smaller and closer together as they recede into the distance.
- **Pixel:** The smallest unit of a digital image, representing a single color value.
- **PNG (Portable Network Graphics):** A raster image format that supports lossless compression and transparency. Often used for web graphics.
- **PPI (Pixels Per Inch):** A measure of image resolution, indicating the number of pixels per inch in an image.
- **PSD (Photoshop Document):** Photoshop's native file format, which preserves layers, adjustments, and other editing information.
- **Puppet Warp:** A tool that allows you to reposition and deform parts of an image by placing and manipulating pins.
- **Quick Mask:** A mode that allows you to create and edit selections using painting tools.
- **Raster Graphics:** Images made up of a grid of pixels. Also known as bitmap images.
- **Rasterize:** To convert vector graphics or text into pixels.
- **Red Eye:** An undesirable effect that often occurs in flash photography when the flash reflects off the subject's retinas, making their eyes appear red.
- **Resampling:** The process of changing the number of pixels in an image when resizing it.
- **Resolution:** The number of pixels per unit of measurement (usually pixels per inch or PPI) in an image.
- **RGB:** An additive color model used for screen display, based on the colors Red, Green, and Blue.
- **Saturation:** The intensity or purity of a color.
- **Scratch Disk:** A designated area on your hard drive that Photoshop uses for temporary storage when it runs out of RAM.
- **Selection:** An area of an image that is isolated for editing.
- **Shadows:** The darkest areas of an image.
- **Sharpen:** To increase the contrast between adjacent pixels, making edges appear more defined.
- **Smart Filter:** A filter applied to a Smart Object that remains editable and non-destructive.
- **Smart Object:** A special type of layer that contains image data from raster or vector images and allows for non-destructive transformations, filtering, and editing.
- **Smoothing:** In the context of brushes, refers to the reduction of jaggedness in brush strokes. In the context of selections, refers to the reduction in the number of angles in a selection.

- **Soft Proofing:** A feature that allows you to preview on your monitor how your image will look when printed.
- **Spot Healing Brush:** A retouching tool that automatically samples the surrounding area to seamlessly remove blemishes and imperfections.
- **Spot Color:** A special premixed ink color used in printing, typically defined using a Pantone color.
- **Straighten:** To correct an image that was taken with a tilted camera, making horizontal or vertical lines appear straight.
- **Stylize:** To apply artistic effects to an image, often simulating traditional art media or creating abstract looks.
- **Swatch:** A saved color sample.
- **Texture:** The visual or tactile surface quality of an object or image. In Photoshop, texture can be simulated using filters or by adding texture overlays.
- **Threshold:** A setting used in various tools and adjustments that determines a cutoff point or boundary. For example, in the Threshold adjustment, it determines which pixels are converted to black and which to white.
- **TIFF (Tagged Image File Format):** A raster image format often used for high-quality printing and archiving. Supports lossless compression and layers.
- **Tolerance:** A setting that determines the range of colors or tones that a tool will select or affect.
- **Tracking:** The adjustment of space between a range of characters in a block of text.
- **Transform:** To change the size, shape, or position of an object or layer. Common transformations include scaling, rotating, skewing, distorting, and applying perspective.
- **Transparency:** The quality of being see-through or partially see-through.
- **Type Tool:** A tool for adding and editing text in Photoshop.
- **Upsampling:** Increasing the number of pixels in an image, often resulting in a loss of sharpness or pixelation.
- **Vanishing Point:** A filter that allows you to work in perspective on an image.
- **Vector Graphics:** Images defined by mathematical equations that describe lines, curves, and shapes. They are resolution-independent and can be scaled without losing quality.
- **Vibrance:** An adjustment that increases the intensity of less saturated colors while having a lesser effect on already saturated colors, helping to prevent oversaturation.
- **Warp:** To distort or reshape an image by manipulating a grid or using preset warp styles.
- **White Balance:** The process of adjusting colors in an image to compensate for the color temperature of the light source, ensuring that white objects appear white.
- **White Point:** The brightest point in an image, representing pure white.
- **Workspace:** A customized arrangement of panels, menus, and tools in Photoshop.
- **Zoom:** To magnify or reduce the view of an image in the document window.

This glossary provides a starting point for understanding common Photoshop terms. As you continue to learn and use Photoshop, you'll undoubtedly encounter more specialized terms, but this list should give you a solid foundation. Remember that you can always refer to the official Adobe Photoshop documentation or other online resources for more detailed information.

www.ingramcontent.com/pod-product-compliance
Lightning Source LLC
LaVergne TN
LVHW081755050326
832903LV00027B/1950